PENGUIN  CL

TREATISE ON TOLERATION

VOLTAIRE was the assumed name of François-Marie Arouet (1694–1778). He was educated at the Jesuit college of Louis-le-Grand, Paris, and studied law briefly before pursuing a career as a writer. He spent two periods locked up in the Bastille before emigrating to England, where he lived from 1726 until 1729; during this period he was influenced by John Locke and Sir Isaac Newton, and by the official toleration of different religions in England. His *Letters concerning the English Nation* (1733) reflect his favourable opinion of English culture and politics, but when a French edition was published clandestinely in France in 1734 it was banned and burned publicly. Often banished from Paris or on the run from threats of arrest, Voltaire spent the years 1734 to 1749 at Cirey in Champagne with his mistress Mme Émilie du Châtelet, with whom he shared many intellectual projects, including the introduction of Newton's physics to France. Famous for his poem in honour of Henri IV, *La Henriade* (1723), for numerous plays that were produced at the Comédie Française, and for his satirical novels, especially *Candide*, Voltaire became the best-known intellectual in Europe and was widely acknowledged to be the voice of the French Enlightenment. The *Treatise on Toleration* (1763) was written as part of his public campaign on behalf of the executed Huguenot shopkeeper Jean Calas, while his *Dictionnaire philosophique portatif* (1764) was more popular than the massive volumes of the *Encyclopédie* (1751–72), to which he also contributed. Following the sudden death of Mme du Châtelet, Voltaire spent time at the court of Frederick the Great in Potsdam, and subsequently lived near Geneva and, from 1759 until his death, near the French–Swiss border at Ferney. He returned briefly to Paris in 1778 for the production of his play *Irène*, and died there on 30 May 1778.

DESMOND M. CLARKE is Emeritus Professor of Philosophy at the National University of Ireland, Cork, and a member of the Royal Irish Academy. His publications include *Descartes's Theory of Mind* (2003), *Descartes: A Biography* (2006) and

The Equality of the Sexes: Three Feminist Texts of the Seventeenth Century (2013); he is also general editor (with Karl Ameriks) of *Cambridge Texts in the History of Philosophy*. He translated two volumes of Descartes's works for Penguin Classics, *Meditations and Other Metaphysical Writings* (1998) and *Discourse on Method and Related Writings* (1999).

VOLTAIRE

Treatise on Toleration

Translated and with an Introduction and Notes by
DESMOND M. CLARKE

PENGUIN BOOKS

PENGUIN CLASSICS

UK | USA | Canada | Ireland | Australia
India | New Zealand | South Africa

Penguin Books is part of the Penguin Random House group of companies
whose addresses can be found at global.penguinrandomhouse.com.

Penguin
Random House
UK

First published in French as *Traité sur la Tolérance, A l'occasion de la
mort de Jean Calas*, 1763
First published in Penguin Classics 2016

016

Introduction, notes and translation copyright © Desmond M. Clarke, 2016
All rights reserved

Set in 10.25/12.25 pt Adobe Sabon
Typeset by Jouve (UK), Milton Keynes
Printed in Great Britain by Clays Ltd, Elcograf S.p.A

ISBN: 978-0-241-23662-8

Contents

TREATISE ON
TOLERATION

Chronology

1694 21 November: Born François-Marie Arouet, in Paris, youngest child of a notary.

1701 Death of his mother.

1704–11 Educated at the Jesuit college of Louis-le-Grand, Paris.

1712 Studies law briefly.

1713 Secretary to the French ambassador in the Netherlands at The Hague; begins an affair with French Protestant refugee Olympe Dunoyer, which leads to his dismissal.

1715 Death of Louis XIV; Philippe, duc d'Orléans becomes Regent of France until 1723, during the minority of Louis XV.

1717–18 Imprisoned in the Bastille for scurrilous writing.

1718 Adopts the name Voltaire; performance of his first tragedy Œdipe.

1721 Death of his father.

1723 Louis XV crowned; publishes *La Ligue*, which is later published (1724) as *La Henriade* (in honour of Henri IV); contracts a near fatal dose of smallpox.

1726–9 Imprisoned briefly in the Bastille, and emigrates to London, where he meets Congreve, Samuel Clarke, Bolingbroke, Pope, reads Swift, and is influenced by Locke and Newton.

1729 Returns to France, lives briefly in Dieppe.

1729–30 Joins with others to buy all the monthly tickets in the Paris lottery and becomes very rich.

1733 *Letters concerning the English Nation* published in London.

1734 French edition of the *Letters* published clandestinely by two different printers as *Lettres philosophiques*, which is condemned and burned by the *parlement* of Paris. Goes to live at Cirey in Champagne with his mistress Mme Émilie du Châtelet.

1738 Publishes a clandestine edition of *Éléments de la philosophie de Newton*.

1740–48 War of the Austrian Succession; concludes with the Treaty of Aix-la-Chapelle.

1741 Voltaire's play *Le Fanatisme, ou Mahomet le Prophète* is produced in Lille.

1743–5 In favour with the royal court, appointed Royal Historian (1745).

1746 Elected member of the Académie française and appointed Gentleman in Ordinary to the King.

1748 The novel *Zadig, ou la Destinée* published.

1749 Mme du Châtelet dies of puerperal fever, following the birth of her daughter.

1750–53 At the court of Frederick the Great.

1751 Publishes *Le Siècle de Louis XIV*, a history of the king's reign.

1755 Settles at Les Délices, near Geneva.

1756 Publishes *Essai sur les mœurs*.

1759 Publishes *Candide, ou l'Optimisme*; moves to Ferney, near the French–Swiss border.

1762 Begins the public campaign to rehabilitate the executed Huguenot shopkeeper Jean Calas.

1763 Publishes *Traité sur la tolérance*.

1764 Publishes *Dictionnaire philosophique portatif*.

1765 English translation of the *Dictionnaire* published as *The Philosophical Dictionary for the Pocket*

1766 Publishes a commentary on the Italian criminologist Cesare Beccaria's *Dei delitti e delle pene* (On Crimes and Punishments).

1767 Publishes his novella *L'Ingénu*.

1774 Death of Louis XV, succeeded by Louis XVI.

1778 Returns to Paris for the first production of his last tragedy *Irène*; dies there on 30 May. Buried in Champagne, but in 1791 his remains are later transferred to the Panthéon in Paris.

Introduction

> 'The law of intolerance is ... absurd and
> barbaric'
>
> (Chapter 6)

Voltaire composed the *Traité sur la tolérance* (*Treatise on Toleration*) in response to a monstrous miscarriage of justice in France. Jean Calas was a Huguenot shopkeeper who lived in a predominantly Catholic area of Toulouse. When one of Jean's sons committed suicide in the family home in October 1761, all the members of the family who were present that evening (together with an overnight visitor) were accused of having murdered him. Convicted of murder, Calas was tortured and executed on 10 March 1762, while the other accused were given less severe sentences.

Voltaire was then sixty-seven years old and living far from Toulouse on the French–Swiss border. He was out of favour with the royal court and had been threatened frequently with arrest warrants, so he had to be able to escape across the border to the Republic of Geneva (where he had lived previously) if the police came to arrest him.

His initial reaction to news of Jean Calas's execution was sceptical and dismissive. He was soon convinced, however, that the judgement of the Toulouse *parlement* was unsafe and that Calas had been wrongly convicted. Once informed about the details of the trial and execution, Voltaire's concerns focused on the religious hostility of Catholics in Toulouse that provoked the verdict rather than on the gruesome cruelty of its implementation. The hatred of one group of French Christians for another was a pessimistic reminder of the wars of religion that had racked the kingdom of France in the sixteenth century and it reawakened Voltaire's interest in a theme that he had discussed almost thirty years earlier in his *Letters concerning the English Nation* (1733).

When the French edition of the *Letters* (1734) was published, the printer was arrested and the Paris *parlement* ordered that the scandalous book be burned publicly. The reasons were obvious. The *Letters* praised various features of public life in England and, by implication, criticized the corresponding political and religious situation in France. They contrasted the simple faith of Quakers with the theological sophistry of the Catholic tradition; the toleration of Calvinists (Presbyterians) in London with the persecution of other Calvinists (Huguenots) in France; and the parliamentary limitations on royal powers in England with the absolute sovereignty claimed by the French crown. In more general terms, the *Letters* praised the innovative and creative energy of British scientific and political opinions in contrast with the conservative tyranny that resulted from the close co-operation between the Catholic Church and the royal court in France.

Although Voltaire subsequently devoted many years, in the company of Mme du Châtelet, to studying and promoting Newton's scientific discoveries as an antidote to what he perceived as the metaphysical dreams of Descartes and Malebranche, he refrained from overt public criticisms of the French establishment after 1734. The Calas trial, however, reignited the powerful emotions he had felt in the 1730s. If an innocent Huguenot could be so unjustly tortured and executed at the instigation of a Catholic mob in Toulouse, then no one was safe and it was time to re-examine the laws and customs of France that discriminated systematically against the Huguenot minority.

Once his anger was roused, Voltaire began to write to influential friends in Paris to seek support for his campaign, and, by the end of 1762, he had drafted a short essay on religious toleration that was printed in April 1763. Although he called it a 'treatise', Voltaire's relatively brief essay on toleration lacked most of the features that were traditionally associated with a treatise: it was not a scholarly, comprehensive and objective summary of the state of knowledge on a given subject. The *Treatise* was much more like the work of a campaigning journalist, and it focused primarily on the way in which French Catholics treated fellow citizens who were Calvinists.

In the course of expressing alarm at the absurdity or irrationality of the openly hostile relations between these two Christian churches in France, Voltaire referred to the prior work of one of his favourite authors, the English philosopher John Locke (1632–1704), who had written a famously brief and radical *Letter concerning Toleration* (1689) when he was living in exile in the United Provinces of the Netherlands. Locke's *Letter* appeared anonymously, as did Voltaire's *Treatise*, and was widely condemned at the time by ecclesiastical authorities.

LOCKE ON TOLERATION

Locke addressed explicitly a question that remains central to church–state relations in modern times, namely: what competence or jurisdiction may civil powers exercise in relation to the religious beliefs and rituals of citizens? His answer – with some obvious qualifications – was: none. This was based partly on his theory of the source and scope of the powers of a state, and partly on his understanding of what is meant by a church.

Locke argued, in the *Second Treatise of Government* (1690), that kings did not receive their jurisdiction directly from God but from the consent of the citizens over whom they exercised political power. He proposed the radically novel theory that human beings are naturally free and equal, and that they possess various fundamental rights that they agree to limit in compensation for the benefits of living in a properly ruled and administered civil society. The assumed benefits of a peaceful commonwealth include the protection of each individual's property, the punishment of those who breach the civil rights of others and access to impartial judges who resolve disputes in accordance with laws that apply to all citizens equally. Therefore, the legislative and judicial powers that are exercised in the name of citizens by the rulers of a state are determined by the objectives for the achievement of which the citizens agree to restrict the exercise of their natural liberties.

It is obvious, according to this theory of a state, that those who govern it have no authority to decide any of the theological issues about which churches may dispute. One reason is that individual citizens have no right to interfere in the religious beliefs of others and, since they lack such authority, they cannot confer it on their rulers. The number of citizens who belong to a given church, therefore, is irrelevant to deciding the scope of religious toleration; the mere fact that a majority of citizens belong to one church rather than another could not confer on political leaders a competence that they naturally lack or a jurisdiction that the citizens are incapable of conferring on them.

In parallel with this account of the source and limits of a state's powers, Locke defined a church as any free association of citizens whose religious beliefs are sufficiently similar to support common rituals or other expressions of their beliefs. Any group of citizens is therefore entitled to establish a church, define the rules for membership and expel those who breach the agreed rules. That concept of a church was reflected in the Constitution of Carolina (1669), which Locke drafted and Voltaire acknowledged in the *Treatise*. The legitimate powers of church members, therefore, complement those of political rulers – they are never entitled to exercise the legislative and judicial powers that are reserved to the state, in the same way that political leaders or institutions of the state may not encroach on the activities of church members as long as they comply with civil law.

Locke thus discussed religious toleration from the point of view of a state's legitimate authority in relation to churches and their members. The only reason for granting legislative and judicial powers to civil rulers was to protect the property and civil rights of citizens and to resolve disputes impartially. Once a state legislates within those limits – which are not easy to define – it may then require all citizens equally to observe its laws and may compel those who refuse to comply.

RELIGIOUS TOLERATION IN FRANCE

When Voltaire was writing his *Treatise* he had not developed an explicit political theory of the state, nor had he endorsed that of Locke. He had devoted most of his life to literary and historical writings, although he had also revealed his sympathies for the English system of government in his *Letters concerning the English Nation*. When he heard about the Calas case, therefore, his primary focus was a theme that he had discussed previously on many occasions: the manifest irrationality of those who held such strong religious convictions that they were willing to kill or torture those who held alternative beliefs. That perspective was very much influenced by the history of France since the sixteenth century.

Jean Calvin (1509–64), rather than Martin Luther, was the leading figure who defined the theology and religious practices of reformed Christians in France during the Reformation. Calvin was forced to emigrate from his native land and to seek refuge in Geneva, where he established the Reformed Church and from the protection of which he spread the message of Christian renewal throughout France. Once the number of Huguenots (as French Calvinists were called) was sufficiently large to constitute a challenge to the political and religious hegemony of the Catholic Church, it was only a matter of time before their religious differences were expressed in political hostility and eventually in civil war.

One of the reasons for this was a fundamental belief that the Catholic and Reformed churches shared, namely that it was impossible for individuals to gain eternal salvation without being a member of the 'true' church.[1] When combined with independent beliefs about one's duties to others and an obligation to protect the divinity from misguided worship, this was transformed into what might be called the logic of the Inquisition, which involved the following elements: the paternalistic coercion of non-members to join the one 'true' church in which alone they could achieve salvation, and the policing of non-members so that they refrain from insulting God by participating in unorthodox religious services. Those who possessed the 'truth' about God and the religious worship that He demands believed that they should force others to accept it or, at least, to refrain from blasphemy or sacrilegious practices.

In addition to this kind of paternalistic coercion, both Catholic and Calvinist theologians claimed a right to kill heretics to protect their own members from losing the faith. Thus St Thomas Aquinas (1225–74), one of the leading theologians in the Roman Catholic tradition, famously argued that the loss of a Christian's eternal life (due to apostasy) was a much greater harm than the loss of a heretic's earthly life and that the latter was a price worth paying to avoid the former.[2] Both churches also argued that they were entitled to request support from civil authorities to implement this kind of religious apartheid. Thus Calvin infamously endorsed the execution of Michael Servetus, who was burned at the stake in Geneva (1553) because he rejected some Calvinist religious doctrines; Cardinal Robert Bellarmine, a Jesuit who was writing in Rome, subsequently cited this execution to confirm his own opinion that a Catholic state is justified in punishing heretics (i.e., Calvinists), even with the death penalty.[3] The two churches were thus symmetrically intolerant of each other and claimed that civil powers should enforce their reciprocal intolerance by penal laws.

The stakes were raised significantly when members of the Reformed Church also claimed a right to defend themselves against the tyranny of 'heretical' civil powers and, if necessary, to kill an heretical king.[4] Catholic theologians argued in parallel that the Pope was entitled to relieve Catholic citizens of their obligation to obey Protestant political rulers. When various noble houses disputed claims to inherit the French crown and supported one or other of the two main Christian churches, conditions were ripe for the religious wars of the sixteenth century, in the course of which thousands of Christians were killed and both sides were responsible for numerous massacres and atrocities. The St Bartholomew's Day Massacre, which began on 23–24 August 1572 and continued for months, in the course of which thousands of Huguenots were murdered by forces loyal to the crown, served as the most notorious example of a pattern that was frequently repeated.

Although Voltaire was writing two centuries later, the underlying issue of religious intolerance had not been resolved in France. Throughout this period Huguenots constituted a minority of the French population. The religious and political question of toleration, therefore, was framed by the Catholic majority in France as follows: what degree of religious freedom should we concede to heretics who represent a permanent threat (for example, by their preaching and public church services) to the faith of Catholic citizens and to the peace of a commonwealth that is predominantly Catholic?

Henri IV (1553–1610), who had been a Calvinist prior to his coronation (when he converted to Catholicism), granted Huguenots limited religious freedom in the Edict of Nantes in 1598. Louis XIV (1638–1715), however, revoked even these modest concessions in 1685. France then reverted to a situation in which it was illegal to practise a reformed version of Christianity and in which the centralized monarchy, in collaboration with the majority church, no longer thought it was politically necessary to grant freedom of worship and practice to a minority of French citizens. As a result, Huguenots emigrated in their thousands to the United Provinces, to Geneva, and to England and Ireland, where they enjoyed enough freedom to practise their religion and to engage in the trades and commercial activities that Voltaire identified as a major economic loss to France.

This official intolerance of Huguenots in France continued into the eighteenth century. While the civil wars that plagued the kingdom during the sixteenth century had abated, the royal court and the professions were staffed almost exclusively by people who were officially Catholic. Even among Catholics, however, there were unresolved public and bitter religious disputes, most notably between Jansenists and their critics. Jansenists favoured a theory of salvation and predestination that had much in common with Calvinism. Since they also shared the political theory of Calvin – to the effect that kings exercise political power merely as a result of original sin, as God's punishment of mankind for the offence of Adam, rather than because of some natural superiority by virtue of which they deserve to rule – Louis XIV and his successors, and polite society in France, considered them almost as objectionable and politically subversive as their counterparts in the Reformed Church. The Jesuits were prominent opponents of Jansenism, but their allegiance to the papacy alienated them from the French episcopate, whose members staunchly defended the independence of the Gallican Church from Rome. Among Catholics, therefore, Jansenists, Jesuits and the secular clergy vied for political support from the crown, while they agreed only about the identity of their common religious enemy, the Huguenots.

VOLTAIRE ON RELIGIOUS TOLERATION

Voltaire interpreted the execution of Jean Calas as a symptom of the religious intolerance that had provoked the religious wars of a previous century. Besides, it was not an isolated incident. He became aware of a number of other equally unjust convictions of Huguenots that seemed to have been motivated by religious hatred. Pierre-Paul Sirven had been wrongly accused of killing one of his own children in 1762, but escaped to Geneva before being arrested. Nonetheless, he was tried and convicted in his absence.[5]

Another case that had a much less benign outcome (although it occurred after Voltaire's *Treatise* was published) involved a young Huguenot, Jean-François Lefèvre, Chevalier de la Barre, who was accused with other youths of having disfigured a crucifix displayed on a public bridge. La Barre was arrested on suspicion of having committed blasphemy and sacrilege at Abbeyville on 9 August 1765. When La Barre's house was searched, police found among his possessions a copy of Voltaire's *Dictionnaire philosophique portatif* (Pocket Philosophical Dictionary). He was inevitably found guilty. La Barre was tortured and executed, and his body was burned publicly together with Voltaire's book in July 1766.[6]

What strikes us most forcefully today about these cases is the barbarism of the tortures and executions, even if the accused people had been guilty of a genuine crime. What struck Voltaire, initially at least, was that all of these miscarriages of justice were motivated by Catholics' hatred of their Huguenot fellow citizens, and this provided the theme of a campaign for religious toleration as one of the defining features of the Enlightenment in Europe.

Voltaire's discussion of religious toleration was neither unique nor completely original. As well as Locke in his famous *Letter*, others had argued for toleration, including the French expatriate Huguenot Pierre Bayle (1647–1706). Voltaire was familiar with Bayle's *Dictionnaire historique et critique* (Historical and Critical Dictionary, 1697) in which the author's support for religious toleration is evident, so much so that in Chapter 24 of the *Treatise* Voltaire mocks an author who cites Bayle as a supporter of intolerance. Bayle also published a multi-volume *Commentaire philosophique* (Philosophical Commentary, 1686–8) on one verse of a parable told by Jesus Christ (Luke 14:23) in which uninvited guests are compelled to come to dinner when those who have been invited send apologies.[7]

Religious toleration was also defended by a number of Voltaire's Huguenot contemporaries, from whose works he borrowed without adequate acknowledgement. These included Laurent Angliviel de la Beaumelle's *L'Asiatique tolérant* (The Tolerant Asiatic, 1748), Antoine Court's *Le Patriote français et impartial* (The Impartial French Patriot, 1751) and his son Antoine Court de Gébelin's *Les Toulousaines* (The Toulousians, 1763). These authors all defended the right of Huguenots to practise their religious faith by appealing to the authority of the Bible and the rights of conscience.

However, aside from the fact that their Catholic fellow citizens rejected their biblical interpretations, the arguments of these Huguenot authors were compromised by the revolutionary conclusions to which religious intolerance had pushed their predecessors in the sixteenth century. They had argued, on biblical grounds, that they had a right to defend their faith by force of arms and, if necessary, even to kill a tyrannical or heretical monarch. Since these sentiments were unlikely to persuade Louis XV (1710–74) and his court, Voltaire discreetly avoided linking his arguments with those of his Huguenot contemporaries.

Instead, his *Treatise* offers an historical review of the extent to which previous generations and other cultures addressed the issue of religious toleration. It claims that the Romans never persecuted anyone simply because of their religious or philosophical beliefs. This seems to contradict the extensive lists of martyrs allegedly executed in the early centuries of Christianity. Voltaire argues, however, that many reports in Christian martyrologies are apocryphal, and if some Christians were persecuted it was invariably because they failed to observe some general law that applied to all citizens of the Empire. Likewise, Voltaire suggests that the Jewish tradition, as reported in the Old Testament, was very tolerant of alternative gods and, although God punished the Israelites for breaches of the Mosaic code, He tolerated variations in cults, sacrifices and other religious rituals through which they appeased God's anger or invoked His assistance.

It is not clear, however, why such historical precedents should convince disputing Christians in the eighteenth century. After all, as Voltaire admits, the customs and laws of those ancient peoples were so different from those of France, and the very language in which their histories are described is so difficult to interpret, that even if they had been grossly intolerant, their behaviour could not have provided an acceptable model for French Christians. The *Treatise* concludes, accordingly, in Chapter 12: 'the whole ancient world was so different to ours that one cannot infer any rule of conduct from it. And even if peoples persecuted or oppressed each other because of their religious beliefs in this remote antiquity, we should not imitate that kind of cruelty in the new dispensation of the law of grace.'

Voltaire offers a more persuasive argument when he discusses the teaching of Jesus Christ in Chapter 14. He examines all the passages from the Gospel in which Jesus apparently approved of coercion, such as the parable in which reluctant guests are compelled to attend a banquet. But he finds no evidence that Jesus ever taught his disciples to force people to adopt certain religious beliefs. Since Jesus was condemned to death for disagreeing with the way in which the Judaic tradition was taught and observed in his own day, Voltaire advises his readers: 'if you wish to resemble Jesus Christ, you ought to be martyrs rather than executioners'.

The preaching of Jesus Christ as found in the Gospel also provides one of the fundamental arguments used in the *Treatise*, in which Voltaire distinguishes between the original teaching of the Gospel and the ways in which relatively simple moral ideals have been complicated during the subsequent history of Christianity. One of Voltaire's favourite examples, to which he often refers in the *Treatise* and in other writings, was the dispute at the First Council of Nicaea (325) about the relationship between God the Father and God the Son (or Jesus Christ). The bishops who participated in that council were reacting to the preaching of Arius, who claimed that Jesus Christ was similar to but not identical with God. Since both sides expressed their views within the conceptual limits of ancient Greek, they distinguished between the 'nature' that the three persons of the Trinity were said to share and the 'personhood' that distinguishes them. The difference between those who claimed Christ had the same nature as God (a view that prevailed as the orthodox teaching expressed in the Athanasian Creed) and those who believed Christ was merely similar to God was reduced to a single letter, 'i', in two Greek words that summarized the alternative doctrines: *homoousian* and *homoiousian*. Even when the Arian controversy was resolved in favour of the divinity of Christ, however, there were further Trinitarian disputes about how to describe the relationship between the Holy Spirit and the Son of God and whether the concept of 'proceeding' is appropriate to describe that relationship.

The history of Christianity is replete with similar theological disputes, many of which are cited by Voltaire as examples of changes in Christian doctrine. One of the most intractable and acrimonious disagreements concerned the interpretation of the words 'This is my body', which were attributed to Jesus Christ at the Last Supper and were then used in commemorations of that event in the sacrament of the Eucharist. Calvinists were unanimous in their conviction that Christ's presence in the Eucharist is symbolic or spiritual, while the Council of Trent (1545–63) had taught that Christ is literally and corporeally present in every sacramental celebration of the Eucharist.[8]

Given the extent of religious disagreement between different Christian sects and the fatal consequences that resulted from attempts to resolve them by force, one might have expected Voltaire to reflect more explicitly on the relative uncertainty of the disputed biblical evidence on which competing doctrines were based. John Locke had addressed that question in a number of works, with which Voltaire was familiar and of which he claimed to be a sympathetic admirer. But Voltaire rarely engaged in systematic philosophical analysis. He does point out in the *Treatise*, however, that it is very difficult after many centuries to understand texts that were originally written in languages that most Christians could no longer read and that may have been corrupted in their transmission by copyists. For example, the title 'son of God' seems to have been used in the Old Testament (although Voltaire did not read Hebrew) to mean someone who was dear to God rather than someone who was literally His son.

The history of Christianity includes so many accretions from scholastic theology (which Voltaire called 'rust') that had been added to the simple words of Scripture that any use of coercion to impose detailed religious beliefs on others would imply a very dangerous principle. If those who hold the so-called orthodox or official doctrine are justified in persecuting those who disagree with them, it would mean that the Romans were justified in crucifying Jesus Christ and that whenever the Catholic Church modified its doctrine it could reclassify as heretical those who held an alternative, earlier version of what it subsequently adopted as its official teaching. 'If Catholics were to say that it is a crime not to believe in the dominant religion,' Voltaire argues, 'that would simply amount to accusing the first Christians, who were their own ancestors, and justifying those whom they accuse of having delivered them to be executed.'[9]

The solution Voltaire proposes to French Catholics in his *Treatise*, therefore, is to 'tolerate' the allegedly mistaken religious beliefs of those whom he describes as 'our errant neighbours who pray to God in bad French'. He had praised the toleration of Catholics in England in the *Letters concerning the English Nation*, despite acknowledging that Catholics and Nonconformists were legally disbarred from holding public offices that were reserved for members of the Church of England. He now recommends, in Chapter 4 of the *Treatise*, that similar qualified liberties should be extended to Huguenots in France. For example, they should be allowed return from exile abroad; their marriages should be recognized; their property rights should be respected and they should not be persecuted simply because of their religious beliefs. The underlying assumption that Huguenots held false religious beliefs (to which their orthodox Catholic neighbours should extend forbearance) is consistent with Voltaire's comment that Jews are destined for eternal damnation, a fate that they could easily avoid by conversion to Christianity.[10]

Although these comments and the general perspective adopted in the *Treatise* might suggest that Voltaire shares the same religious views as the Catholics he addresses, he intentionally camouflaged his personal religious beliefs. He was brought up as a Roman Catholic and attended one of the most renowned Jesuit colleges in Paris, the Collège Louis-le-Grand. During the course of his life, however, he was persuaded that the theological subtleties that distinguished churches or religions from each other were more like superstitions than genuine knowledge, and that they were mere culturally relative expressions of a fundamental philosophical belief in God as creator of the universe. Thus Voltaire adopted a form of Unitarianism that was similar to that of Locke and Newton, which rejected belief in a Trinitarian divinity. Since that was hardly less objectionable in France than Calvinism, and since Voltaire was pleading publicly with those who governed the kingdom, the *Treatise* was written – for rhetorical reasons – as if its author were an orthodox Catholic discussing with other Catholics how, as Christians, they ought to deal with the existence in France of a significant minority of dissenting 'heretics'.

'Toleration', in this context, therefore, assumes that those who practise toleration have true beliefs and morally superior standards of behaviour, and that the subjects of their forbearance are misguided and potentially endanger the beliefs and practices of their tolerant fellow citizens. In a word, Catholics are right and Huguenots are wrong, and toleration need extend no further than to refrain from forcing Huguenots to share the same religious beliefs and practices as their neighbours. But Voltaire does not argue, at this time, that Huguenots should enjoy exactly the same civil and political rights as Catholics. He is merely inviting the majority church in France not to persecute or kill members of a minority Christian church.

This exclusive focus on relations between two Christian churches in France reflects a political judgement that Voltaire had made in Letter 6 (On the Presbyterians) in his *Letters concerning the English Nation*, and which he repeated in the *Treatise*:

> If there were only one religion in England there would be danger of despotism, if there were two they would cut each other's throats, but there are thirty, and they live in peace and happiness.[11]

There were only two Christian churches in eighteenth-century France, both of them affiliated with prominent noble families that aspired to political office and, according to Voltaire's estimate, Huguenots constituted less than 10 per cent of the population. His plea for toleration in the *Treatise*, therefore, is directed at the other 90 per cent. It is an argument that relies on the benefits to the nation that would result from a policy of toleration – not only peaceful co-existence between members of different churches but also an enhanced national defence against external enemies and a significantly improved economy. Besides, a limited degree of toleration is consistent with the doctrine of the Gospel which the majority of French citizens claimed to believe.

THE SACRED AND THE SECULAR

One of the fundamental issues that arises in Voltaire's *Treatise*, and which remains central to all modern discussions, is the source and status of the values by reference to which a state formulates policies concerning religious toleration and freedom of thought. There are no neutral values to which one might appeal. The primary question, then, is whether the values on which a state relies to support public policy are religious values that vary from one church to another or are independent of (or at least common to) the diverse religious beliefs of its citizens.

Those who base their political decisions on God's revelation usually assume the certainty of their religious beliefs without questioning the credibility of the evidence that supports them. For example, if a people believe that God chose them as His special nation and granted them a geographical territory as their earthly home, they are likely to wage war to capture and hold what God had allegedly given them. If other people believe that God granted them the same land and told them to hold it for their exclusive use, then both sides will appeal to their incompatible religious beliefs and neither side is likely to accept that mere human laws or conventions may outweigh the moral authority of divine commands. For that reason, Locke and Voltaire not only condemn the barbarism of murdering others for religious reasons, but they invite all religious believers to reflect on the uncertainty of the evidence on which their beliefs rest.

When people hold incompatible religious beliefs and rely on those beliefs to support legal or political claims against others, Locke asks 'by what right' does one church claim authority over others? The standard response is that 'the orthodox church has this right against the erroneous or heretical church', to which Locke answers: 'Every church is orthodox in its own eyes, and in the eyes of others it is erroneous or heretical.'[12]

Voltaire invites readers of the *Treatise* to consider a similar argument in Chapter 6. If members of a political community accept the reciprocity of moral obligations and consider a principle such as the following: 'Do not do what you would not like someone to do to you', the implications for toleration are obvious. Each religious group or church must grant freedom of thought to others. Otherwise, they would face their fellow citizens with the following demand that cannot be satisfied simultaneously and reciprocally: 'Believe what I believe and what you cannot believe, or you will die.'

It is impossible, therefore, to achieve peaceful relations between incompatible religious traditions unless their members modify either the political implications of their beliefs or the certainty with which they hold them. The first option is to interpret one's religious beliefs as applicable only to oneself. In that case religious beliefs may give meaning to one's existence or console people in distress, but they do not entitle the believer to take any action whatsoever in relation to other citizens. The history of religions shows that this kind of restraint is frequently ignored, especially when people also believe that God has imposed a mission on them to convert – by force if necessary – those whom they classify as heretics. Voltaire reflects on the missionary evangelism of the Jesuits in India and China as an example of compliance with such a divine command, which is understood as no less compulsory or categorical than other religious beliefs.

The offensive or protective dynamic of fundamentalist religious believers – either to force others to share their beliefs or to protect their own faith from contamination by 'heretics' – also leads Voltaire to question the truth of religious beliefs and the evidence on which they are allegedly based. While Locke and Voltaire both support belief in God as the creator of the universe, they both regard the great diversity of religious traditions in the world as alternative cultural expressions of this basic belief.[13] This is an alternative (epistemological) route to religious toleration. It involves questioning the significance and credibility of the detailed doctrines about which religions differ and adopting a general attitude of respect towards the mysterious reality of an infinite universe in comparison with which individual human lives and their petty theological disputes are reduced to trifles.

Accordingly, Voltaire asks his readers to reconsider the foundation of their religious faith. When he reviews theories about the soul's immortality in Chapter 13, he argues that our ignorance about the nature of the human mind is a symptom of a more widespread inability to understand what he calls 'God's secrets'. He concludes: 'All these comments are relevant to the fundamental question whether human beings should tolerate each other. For if they show how much people have been mistaken about different things from time immemorial, they also show that human beings ought to have treated each other with indulgence at all times.' Religious scepticism is one of the familiar arguments in favour of toleration since the time of Locke – the fact that inconsistent claims cannot all be true, and that even a cursory reflection on the variety and incredibility of so many religious beliefs should convince those who adopt them that they lack the kind of certainty that could justify coercing others.

FREEDOM OF THOUGHT

Although Voltaire's plays were often produced at the Comédie Française in Paris, many of his other writings were published clandestinely, without the royal permission that was required in France. As a result, he lived for almost fifty years in exile from Paris – in the United Provinces, England, Champagne, Potsdam, Geneva and finally at Ferney, near the French–Swiss border. He was on the run for decades from ecclesiastical and royal authorities. In the final decades of his life he began to think more systematically about what he called 'freedom of conscience' (Chapter 5) or 'freedom of thought' (Chapter 7), rather than the limited freedom of Huguenots to practise an alternative form of Christianity. He addressed this question explicitly in his pamphlet *Idées républicaines* (Republican Ideas, 1765), in which he argued in favour of the freedom to express one's thoughts:

> In a republic worthy of the name, freedom to publish one's thoughts is a citizen's natural right. They may use a pen or their voice, and should not be prevented from writing any more than speaking . . .

That is the law in England, a monarchical country, where people are freer than elsewhere because they are more enlightened.[14]

Although this demand for freedom of thought was provoked by an apparent abuse of power by the council in Geneva that controlled the civil, political and religious lives of its citizens, Voltaire was beginning to formulate a theory of church–state separation, according to which the very phrase 'a civil and ecclesiastical government' was an insult to reason. One ought to speak instead, he argued, about 'a civil government and ecclesiastical regulations' and to acknowledge that the latter can be made only by civil powers.[15]

Likewise, the first edition of Voltaire's *Pocket Philosophical Dictionary* includes an article on 'Toleration'. Since it was printed clandestinely in Geneva and was predictably banned in France, Voltaire was able to deny authorship, at least initially: 'Luckily I had nothing to do with that nasty work . . . I read that diabolical dictionary; it alarmed me as much as you.'[16] When later, expanded editions appeared, however, and the identity of the author became obvious, Voltaire added an article on 'Freedom of Thought', in which he refers to the people of England who are happy because they enjoy a 'right to express their opinion'.[17] This is also the clear implication of the ironic bafflement of the 'Child of Nature' in *L'Ingénu* (1767), when confronted with theological disputes among his French hosts that could not be found anywhere in the New Testament, on which they claimed to base their faith.

This recognition of a natural right to freedom of thought and religion became one of the defining features of the Enlightenment and was subsequently promulgated in Article 11 of the *Déclaration des droits de l'Homme et du citoyen* (Declaration of the Rights of Man and the Citizen, 1789):

The free communication of ideas and opinions is one of the most precious of human rights; every citizen therefore may speak, write and print freely, although they must account for any abuse of this freedom in specific circumstances that are determined by law.

With this proclamation, revolutionary France acknowledged the fundamental idea that had motivated Voltaire's thesis in the *Treatise*.

Freedom of thought is widely recognized today as a fundamental human right. It is protected, for example, by Article 18 of the United Nations International Covenant on Civil and Political Rights (1966), which states:

> Everyone shall have the right to freedom of thought, conscience and religion. This right shall include freedom to have or to adopt a religion or belief of his choice, and freedom, either individually or in community with others and in public or private, to manifest his religion or belief in worship, observance, practice and teaching.

The UN Covenant acknowledges that this freedom is subject only to limitations that 'are prescribed by law and are necessary to protect public safety, order, health, or morals or the fundamental rights and freedoms of others'.

The articulation and implementation of an appropriate public policy that recognizes the religious freedom of every citizen is a work in progress in most jurisdictions. While the details remain to be resolved, case by case, the fundamental principle on which such resolutions depend is that to which Voltaire contributed significantly in his *Treatise*: that individual citizens have a right to freedom of thought and religious belief, and that states have no authority to interfere in that right except to protect the civil rights of others.

NOTES

1. The Catholic Church taught that 'outside the Church no one can be saved'. See Chapter 22, note 4.
2. *Summa theologiae*, IIaIIae, q. 11, article 3.
3. Robert Bellarmine, *On Temporal and Spiritual Authority*, trans. Stefania Tutino (Indianapolis: Liberty Fund, 2012), p. 102.
4. This theory was developed by the so-called monarchomachs in the sixteenth century, including Théodore de Bèze and François Hotman.

5. Voltaire summarized this case in 'Avis au public sur les parri-
    cides imputés aux Calas et aux Sirven' ('Advice to the Public
    about the Parricides attributed to the Calas and Sirven Fami-
    lies', September 1766), in Voltaire, *Mélanges*, ed. Jacques Van
    den Heuvel (Paris: Gallimard, 1961), pp. 827–47.

6. 'Relation de la mort du chevalier de La Barre' ('An Account of
    the Death of Chevalier de La Barre'), *Mélanges*, pp. 773–85.

7. *Commentaire philosophique sur ces paroles de Jesus-Chrit*
    [*sic*] (1686–8). The gospel phrase 'compel them to come in' was
    used as justification for coercing people to become members of
    various Christian churches.

8. The Council of Trent's Eucharistic theology is summarized in
    Session XIII, *Decrees of the Ecumenical Councils*, 2 vols., ed.
    Norman P. Tanner (London: Sheed & Ward, 1990), pp. 693–8.

9. Voltaire used a similar argument in the article 'Liberté de
    Penser' ('Freedom of Thought') in the *Pocket Philosophical
    Dictionary*, because if the Romans had not allowed freedom to
    practise a different religion, Christianity could never have
    spread throughout the Empire: *Œuvres complètes de Voltaire*
    (Oxford: Voltaire Foundation, 1994), vol. 36, p. 299.

10. Voltaire reports without dissent the belief of his Catholic readers
    that Jews suffer eternal punishment if they fail to convert to Chris-
    tianity, in Chapter 13, p. 86: 'This temporal punishment . . . cannot
    be considered a punishment at all when compared with the eternal
    punishment that results from their incredulity, which they could
    avoid by means of a sincere conversion.'

11. *Letters on England*, trans. Leonard Tancock (London: Pen-
    guin, 2005), p. 41. Voltaire alludes to this in Chapter 5 below,
    where he argues as follows: 'The more sects there are, the less
    dangerous each one of them becomes.'

12. *Locke on Toleration*, ed. Richard Vernon (Cambridge: Cam-
    bridge University Press, 2010), p. 14.

13. For Voltaire's religious beliefs, see René Pomeau, *La Religion
    de Voltaire*, rev. edn (Paris: Librairie Nizet, 1969).

14. *Idées républicaines par un membre d'un corps* (Republican
    Ideas, by a citizen), in Voltaire, *Mélanges*, p. 509.

15. Ibid., p. 506.

16. To Damilaville (9 July 1764), and to d'Alembert (7 September
    1764), D 11978, 12073, in *Correspondence and related docu-
    ments*, ed. Theodore Besterman (Oxford: Voltaire Foundation,
    1969–1977), vols 85–135.

17. *Œuvres complètes*, vol. 36, pp. 294–301 at 300.

Further Reading

The first edition of the *Traité sur la tolérance* is available on the Gallica website of the Bibliothèque nationale de France. There is a modern critical edition edited by John Renwick, which is volume 56C of the *Œuvres complètes de Voltaire* (Oxford: Voltaire Foundation, 2000). The Voltaire Foundation website also includes detailed information about all of Voltaire's publications and the best editions currently available. Many of Voltaire's shorter works are translated in Penguin Classics.

Ian Davidson's *Voltaire: A Life* (London: Profile Books, 2010) is a comprehensive biography based on Voltaire's extensive correspondence.

There were two authors whose work significantly influenced Voltaire's discussion in the *Treatise*, John Locke and Cesare Beccaria. English translations of their work are available as follows: *Locke on Toleration*, ed. Richard Vernon (Cambridge: Cambridge University Press, 2010), which includes a modern English translation of Locke's *Epistola de Tolerantia*; *Beccaria: On Crimes and Punishments and Other Writings*, ed. Richard Bellamy (Cambridge: Cambridge University Press, 1995), which includes an English translation of *Dei delitti e delle pene* (1764). The history of religious wars in France is summarized in Robin Briggs's *Early Modern France 1560–1715*, 2nd edn (Oxford: Oxford University Press, 1998).

Studies devoted specifically to the *Treatise on Toleration* include *Etudes sur le Traité sur la tolérance de Voltaire*, ed. Nicholas Cronk (Oxford: Voltaire Foundation, 2000).

Note on the Text

This translation is based on the Voltaire Foundation edition of the text, *Traité sur la tolérance* (Oxford, 2000), ed. John Renwick; I have borrowed the results of its extensive research on sources mentioned by Voltaire while correcting some of its notes and adding others. I have also translated texts that Voltaire quoted in Latin.

There are two sets of notes in this edition. Voltaire's own notes – some of which are quite long and develop arguments in the main text – have been translated as footnotes. There are also many references or allusions to persons and events in the original text, which are clarified in editorial endnotes at the end of this translation. When Voltaire's footnotes require an editorial clarification, this has been added at the conclusion of the footnote in square brackets, prefixed with the word '*Ed.*' Titles of publications in foreign languages are translated in brackets.

Voltaire's frequent quotations from the Bible raise the question of how best to translate his citations into English. It is clear that he consulted the Vulgate, i.e., the Latin edition of the Bible that was officially adopted within the Catholic Church, although in at least one instance he seems to have consulted the French translation by Louis-Isaac Lemaistre de Sacy, which was known as the *Bible de Port-Royal*. For the most part, therefore, I have quoted from the Douay-Rheims English translation of the Vulgate, except when Voltaire's citations are so loose as to be paraphrases. In those cases I translated his French version directly into English.

TREATISE ON
TOLERATION

ONE

A Brief Account of the Death
of Jean Calas

The murder of Calas, which was committed by the judicial authorities at Toulouse on 9 March 1762, is one of the most momentous events that deserve the attention of our own age and that of posterity. The almost countless masses of dead who perished in battles are soon forgotten, not only because their deaths are an inevitable consequence of war, but because those who died in battles could also have killed their enemies and they did not die without defending themselves. When danger and advantage are thus equal, it is not surprising that even one's sympathy is diminished. But if an innocent father of a family is delivered into the clutches of error, passion or fanaticism; if the accused has no defence apart from his own virtue; if those who pronounce a death sentence risk nothing more than making a mistake by killing him; if they can kill with impunity by a simple decree, then public opinion is outraged and everyone fears for himself or herself. It becomes obvious that no one's life is safe before a court that was established to protect the lives of citizens, and everyone agrees to demand retribution.

This remarkable affair involved religion, suicide and parricide. What had to be decided was whether a father and mother had strangled their son to please God; if one brother had strangled another; if a friend had strangled his friend; and if the judges had reason to reproach themselves for having sentenced an innocent father to death on the wheel or for having spared a guilty mother, brother and friend.

Jean Calas, who was aged sixty-eight,[1] had worked as a merchant in Toulouse for more than forty years, and all his neighbours knew him as a good father. He was a Protestant, as were his wife and all his children, except one who had renounced heresy and to whom his father had granted a modest allowance.[2] Jean Calas seemed to have rejected the absurd fanaticism that sunders the bonds of society to such an extent that he had approved the religious conversion of his son Louis and had employed a zealous Catholic servant[3] in his home for thirty years to take care of all his children.

One of Jean Calas's sons, Marc-Antoine, had been well educated; he was known to have a disturbed, serious and violent disposition. This young man failed to develop a successful career in business, for which he had little natural aptitude, and he also failed to be registered as a lawyer, because he could not obtain the required certificate to show that he was a Catholic. He subsequently decided to take his own life and revealed his decision to one of his friends. He confirmed his resolution by reading everything that was ever written about suicide.

One day, when he had lost money at gambling, Marc-Antoine decided that the day had come to implement his plan. One of his friends,[4] who was also a friend of the family and whose name was Lavaisse – a youth aged nineteen, who was known to be honest and personable, and was the son of a well-known lawyer in Toulouse – had arrived from Bordeaux the previous evening.* He happened to dine with the Calas family that evening. The father, mother, Marc-Antoine (their eldest son) and Pierre (their second son) had a family meal together. After dinner they retired to a small lounge and Marc-Antoine absented himself from the others. Later, when the Lavaisse youth wished to leave, he and Pierre Calas went downstairs and found Marc-Antoine there, dressed in his shirt, hanging from a door near the storeroom. His clothes were folded on a table, his shirt was not even ruffled, his hair was combed well and he had no marks or bruises on his body.†

---

* 12 October 1761.

† When they brought his body to the town hall, they found only a slight scratch at the tip of his nose and a small bruise on his chest that resulted from carelessness as they transported the body.

We omit here all the details that the lawyers released. Nor shall we describe the sorrow and despair of the father and mother, whose cries were heard by their neighbours. Lavaisse and Pierre Calas, who were beside themselves, ran off to call a doctor and notify the magistrate.

While they were doing so, and while the parents were grieving and crying, the people of Toulouse gathered outside the house. They are superstitious and irrational people; they think of fellow citizens who do not share their religious beliefs as if they were monsters. Toulouse is the place where they thanked God solemnly for the death of Henry III, and where they swore to kill the first person who would even mention recognizing the great and good Henry IV.[5] This town still celebrates every year, with processions and bonfires, the anniversary of the massacre of four thousand heretical citizens two centuries ago.[6] Six Council decrees failed to prevent this odious celebration, which the people of Toulouse have always celebrated as if it were a religious festival.

Some fanatic in the crowd shouted that Jean Calas had hanged his son Marc-Antoine. As others repeated this accusation, it very quickly became a unanimous clamour. Some people added that the deceased was about to renounce his Calvinist faith the following day, and that his family and the Lavaisse youth had strangled him because they hated the Catholic religion. Almost immediately, the crowd accepted the rumour as if it were a fact. The whole town was convinced that it was an article of faith for Protestants that a mother and father were obliged to assassinate their son as soon as he decided to convert to Catholicism.[7]

Once passions are aroused, they get out of control very easily. The people of Toulouse imagined that the Protestants of Languedoc had assembled the previous evening and, by a majority vote, had elected an executioner from among members of their sect, that the Lavaisse youth had been selected for that duty, and that the young man had heard the result of his election within twenty-four hours and had then travelled from Bordeaux to assist Jean Calas, his wife and their son Pierre to strangle a friend, son and brother.

Mr David,[8] who was the Presiding Magistrate of Toulouse, was provoked to act on the basis of these rumours and wished to benefit by taking prompt action. Accordingly, he initiated a prosecution that breached all the rules and ordinances. The Calas family, their Catholic housemaid and Lavaisse were all arrested and shackled.

A monitory[9] was also published, which was just as defective as the legal process that had already begun. Matters then got even more out of hand. Since Marc-Antoine had died a Calvinist, if he had committed suicide his body should have been dragged through the streets on a rack. Instead, he was buried with extravagant ceremony in the Church of St Stephen, despite the fact that the curate protested against this profanation of consecrated ground.

There are four confraternities of penitents in Languedoc, the so-called White, Blue, Grey and Black Penitents. Their members wear a long hood and a linen cover over their heads with two holes through which they can see. They tried to persuade the Duke of Fitz-James,[10] who was governor of the province, to join their confraternity but he refused. The members of the white confraternity provided the kind of solemn funeral for Marc-Antoine that would have been appropriate for a martyr. No church had ever celebrated the feast of a genuine martyr with greater pomp; but on this occasion, the display was appalling. They placed a moving skeleton on top of a magnificent catafalque, which represented Marc-Antoine holding a palm in one hand and, in the other, a quill with which he was supposed to have recanted his heresy and which effectively signed his father's death warrant.

The unfortunate victim of suicide lacked nothing short of being officially canonized. All the people regarded him as a saint. Some of them invoked his intercession and others prayed at his tomb; others requested that he perform miracles, while still others told stories about miracles that he had already performed. A monk extracted some teeth from the corpse to save as permanent relics. One devout woman, who was slightly deaf, said she heard the sound of church bells. An apoplectic priest was cured after taking an emetic. Reports were prepared about these extraordinary events. This author possesses an affidavit to the effect that a young man from Toulouse went insane after praying for many nights at the tomb of the new saint without obtaining the miracle that he had requested.

Some of the magistrates were members of the confraternity of the White Penitents. That fact alone made the death of Jean Calas almost inevitable.

Above all else, what sealed his fate was the fact that they were approaching the date of the strange festival at which the people of Toulouse celebrated annually the massacre of four thousand Huguenots, and 1762 was the bicentenary of that event. The decorations for that solemn celebration were erected in the town, and those alone further inflamed the overwrought imagination of its citizens. It was said publicly that the scaffold on which the Calas family would be executed would be the greatest ornament of the festivities. It was said that Providence itself had led these victims to be sacrificed to our holy religion. Twenty witnesses heard these reports and other comments that were even more violent. And that all happened in our own day – and during a period when philosophy had made so much progress! And it occurred while a hundred academies studied to promote a spirit of gentleness in civil life! It seems as if fanaticism, which had been affronted by the success of Reason in the recent past, struggled even more angrily under the yoke of rationality.

Thirteen judges held meetings every day to decide the case. There was no evidence – and it was impossible to have had any evidence – against the family, but a misguided religion provided a substitute. Six of the judges continued to condemn Jean Calas, his son and Lavaisse to be executed on the wheel, and to condemn Jean Calas's wife to be burned at the stake. Seven other more moderate judges wanted at least to hear the evidence. The discussions between both groups were repetitious and lengthy. One of the judges, who was convinced that all the accused were innocent and that the crime could not possibly have been committed, spoke strongly in their favour. He opposed the zeal of harsh justice with the zeal of human kindness. He became the public defender of the Calas family in all the houses of Toulouse where the unrelenting demands of an exploited religion sought the blood of these unfortunate people. Another judge, who had a reputation for violence, spoke in the town with as much passion against the Calas family as the former judge had displayed in their defence. Eventually, the confrontation between the two judges was so intense that both of them had to recuse themselves and they retired to the country.

Unfortunately, however, the judge who was favourable to the Calas family had the integrity to persist in recusing himself, while the other judge returned to vote against people whom he ought never to have judged. His vote was decisive in condemning them to the wheel, because the final decision was only eight votes to five, and one of the judges who had opposed the sentence changed his mind at the last minute, after many arguments, and voted with the harsher judges.[11]

In cases of alleged parricide, when the father of a family is to be delivered to the most appalling penalty, it seems as if the decision ought to be unanimous because the proof for such an unusual* crime should be so solid that the evidence would convince everyone. The slightest doubt in a case such as this should

* I know of only two cases in history where a father was accused of having assassinated his child for religious reasons. The first was the father of St Barbara (whom we call a saint). He had installed two windows in the bathroom but, while he was absent, Barbara installed a third window in honour of the Holy Trinity. She also made the sign of the cross on the marble columns with the tip of her finger, which became deeply engraved on the columns. Her father was so angry that he chased her with his sword, but she escaped through a mountain that opened up to receive her. Her father circled around the mountain and captured her. She was flogged, completely naked, but God clothed her with a white cloud. Finally, her father decapitated her. That is how it is reported in the *Flower of the Saints*. The second example was Prince Hermengild. He revolted against his father, the king, and joined battle with him in 584, in the course of which he was defeated and killed by an officer. He was recognized as a martyr because his father was an Arian. [*Ed.* St Barbara was killed by her father *c.* 235 because she refused to renounce her Christianity. *Flower of the Saints* was written by a Spanish Jesuit, Pedro de Ribadeneira (1527–1611), and was translated into French in the seventeenth and eighteenth centuries, although Voltaire could hardly have endorsed its historical accuracy. Prince Hermengild was the son of the king of the Visigoths and refused to renounce his Christianity.]

be enough to stay the hand of any judge who is about to sign a death sentence. We experience on a daily basis the weakness of our reason and the inadequacy of our laws, but does anything demonstrate their fragility more clearly than a citizen being condemned to the wheel by a majority decision of a single vote? In Athens they required fifty votes more than half before they dared to impose a death sentence. And what do we learn from that? Something that we already know, while failing to learn anything from it: that the Greeks were wiser and more humane than we are.

It seemed impossible that Jean Calas, who was an old man of sixty-eight and had suffered from weak, swollen legs for a long time, could have strangled and hanged his twenty-eight-year-old son without assistance, since his son was stronger than average for his age. He certainly would have needed to be assisted in doing so by his wife, by his son Pierre Calas, by Lavaisse and also by his housemaid. On the evening of the fatal event these people were never separated from each other for a single moment. But that assumption is even more absurd than the previous one, for how could a zealous Catholic serv- ant have allowed Huguenots to assassinate a young man whom she had cared for as a child in order to punish him for having loved the same religion that she herself professed? How could Lavaisse have arrived from Bordeaux with the intention of strangling his friend, even though he was not even aware of his alleged religious conversion? How could a loving mother have laid hands on her own son? How could they have been able jointly to strangle a young man who was as strong as all of them together without a long and violent struggle, without ter- rible cries that would have alerted their neighbours, without repeated blows to the victim and without any bruises or torn clothing?

It was evident that, if it had been possible to commit parri- cide, then all the accused would have been equally guilty, because they had been together during the whole evening. It was obvious that they were not all guilty. It was equally obvi- ous that the father alone could not have been guilty; and yet the verdict condemned only the father to die on the wheel.

The reason for this verdict was just as incomprehensible as everything else. The judges who decided that Jean Calas should be executed convinced the other judges that this weak old man would not be able to endure torture, and that he would confess his own crime and that of his accomplices once the executioner began to torture him. They were therefore confounded when this old man, as he was dying on the wheel, asked God to testify to his innocence and implored Him to pardon his judges.

The judges were then forced to issue a second verdict,[12] which contradicted the first one. They decided that the mother, her son Pierre, Lavaisse and the housemaid should be released. But when one of the counsellors pointed out that this judgement contradicted the first one – and that the judges thereby condemned themselves, because all of the accused had been in each other's company during the whole time when the parricide was supposed to have occurred, and that the release of the survivors proved beyond all doubt the innocence of the condemned father of the family – they decided instead to send his son Pierre into exile. This banishment was as irrational and absurd as everything that preceded it, because Pierre Calas was either guilty of parricide or he was innocent. If he was guilty, he should have been broken on the wheel like his father; if he was innocent, he should not have been exiled. But the judges were so moved by the father's suffering and the touching piety with which he had died that they thought they could salvage their reputation by giving the impression that they were being merciful to the son, as if being 'merciful' was not another example on their part of failing to comply with the law. They believed that banishing this poor young man, who had no resources, would be a trivial thing because it was not very unjust in comparison with the injustice that they had already unfortunately committed.

They began by threatening Pierre Calas, when he was in his prison cell, that they would treat him in the same way as they had dealt with his father if he refused to renounce his religion. That is what the young man reported in a sworn affidavit.*

* 'A Dominican came to my cell and threatened me with the same death as my father if I did not convert. I swear this before God, 23 July 1762. Pierre Calas.'

When Pierre Calas was leaving the town he met a priest who specialized in religious conversions and who made him return to Toulouse. They locked him up in a Dominican priory and forced him to observe all the religious duties of the Catholic faith.[13] That was partly what they hoped to achieve, as the price of his father's blood, and the religion that they hoped to avenge seemed to have been appeased.

The Calas daughters were taken from their mother and confined to a convent. This woman, almost drenched in her husband's blood, who had held her son's corpse in her arms and had seen her other son exiled, who was deprived of her daughters and stripped of all her possessions, was left alone in the world without food, without hope and dying from extreme suffering. A few people, who reflected dispassionately on all the circumstances of this appalling event, were so struck by it that they encouraged the Calas widow – who had retired into solitude – to have the courage to appeal to the king. She was unable to do so, however, because she was gradually getting weaker. Besides, since she was born in England and had emigrated to a French province at a young age, the very mention of Paris frightened her. She imagined that the capital of the kingdom would be even more barbarous than Toulouse. Eventually, however, the duty to avenge the memory of her husband overcame her weakness. She was close to death when she arrived in Paris. She was surprised to be welcomed there, and to be offered assistance and sympathy.

Reason is stronger than fanaticism in Paris, no matter how great the latter is, whereas in the provinces fanaticism is almost always more powerful than reason.

Mr de Beaumont, a renowned lawyer of the Paris *parlement*,[14] initially accepted the brief for her defence and prepared a submission that was signed by fifteen lawyers. Mr Loiseau, who was equally distinguished, composed a summary of the case in support of the family. Mr Mariette, who was a member of the Judicial Council, prepared an appeal that won the approval of the public.

These three generous defenders of justice and innocence assigned to the widow all the income they earned by

publishing their legal submissions.* Paris and the whole of
Europe were moved to pity her and demanded justice for this
unfortunate woman. The public had already announced its
own verdict long before the Council could have made their
decision.

Sympathy reached into the very heart of government, despite
the unrelenting demands of normal business, which usually
exclude all such emotions, and despite the fact that the people
who were involved in government were used to seeing misfortune, which can harden the heart even more than usual. The
daughters were returned to their mother, and they were seen –
all three of them – clothed in black veils and bathed in tears,
which provoked their judges to cry with them.

Meanwhile, this family still had some enemies, because religion was involved. Several of those people who are described
as 'devout' in France† expressed the view publicly that it
would be better to put an old, innocent Huguenot to death on
the wheel than to force eight judges in Languedoc to admit
that they had made a mistake. They even used the slogan
'There are more judges than Calases', from which they concluded that the Calas family should have been sacrificed to
protect the reputation of the judiciary. They failed to realize
that the reputation of judges, like that of anyone else, is determined by whether or not they correct their mistakes. In France,
people do not generally believe that the Pope is infallible when
he decides matters with the agreement of his cardinals.[15] One
would think that, for similar reasons, eight judges in Toulouse
are not infallible either. Every sensible, impartial observer was
already saying that it would have been possible to quash the
Toulouse verdict in any other place in Europe, even if there
were local factors in Paris that prevented the Council from
granting the appeal.

* The publications were pirated in many towns and the widow Calas was
deprived of the benefits of their generosity.
† The French term *dévot* comes from the Latin *devotus*. The devout of
ancient Rome were those who dedicated themselves to the safety of the
Republic, such as the Curtii and the Decii.

That was how matters stood in this extraordinary affair when a number of sensible, impartial people conceived a plan to publish reflections on toleration, clemency and compassion, which Father Houtteville[16] calls a 'monstrous dogma' in his inflated and misguided rant about facts, but which Reason describes as the rightful inheritance of humanity.

Either the judges of Toulouse, encouraged by the fanaticism of the mob, caused an innocent man to be executed on the wheel, which was unprecedented, or this father of a family and his wife strangled their eldest son and were assisted in that parricide by another one of their sons and by his friend, which is an unnatural crime. In either case, an abuse of the most holy religion caused a great crime. It is therefore in the interests of humanity to examine whether religion should be charitable or barbarous.

TWO

Consequences of the Execution
of Jean Calas

If the White Penitents caused an innocent man to be executed, the complete ruin of a family, the scattering of its members and the public disgrace that ought to be reserved for injustice, especially if it results in death by torture; if the White Penitents honoured, as if he were a saint, someone who ought to have been drawn through the streets, and if their haste in doing so caused a virtuous father of a family to be tortured on the wheel, this evil deed should certainly have made them genuine penitents for the rest of their lives and, together with the judges in this case, they ought to weep – but without a long white habit and a mask over their heads that would hide their tears.

All these confraternities deserve our respect and are salutary. But no matter how great the benefit they may confer on the State, how could one compare it with the appalling evil that they have caused? They seem to be inspired by the same zeal that motivates Catholics in Languedoc against the people whom we call Huguenots. It seems as if they took a vow to hate their fellow citizens, because we have enough religion to hate and persecute others, but not enough to love and support them. And what would happen if these confraternities were governed by the kind of enthusiasts who controlled certain associations of artisans and titled people long ago, who turned the custom of seeing visions into an art form and a regular occurrence, as reported by one of our most eloquent and wise magistrates?[1] What would happen if the confraternities had set up darkened rooms similar to the so-called 'meditation rooms', which were decorated with images of devils armed with horns and claws, flaming abysses, crosses and daggers, and with the holy name of Jesus at the top of the whole scene? What a spectacle that would be for eyes that are already spellbound and for imaginations that are as fertile as they are obedient to those who manipulate them!

We know very well that there were times when these confraternities were dangerous. The Brothers and Flagellants caused a lot of mischief. The League began with similar members. Why would they have distinguished themselves in that way from other citizens? Did they think they were more perfect than others? That alone is an insult to the rest of the nation. Did they want all Christians to join a confraternity?[2] That would be a wonderful spectacle – the whole of Europe dressed in hoods and masks, with two small round holes for their eyes to peer through! Does anyone really believe that God prefers such clothes to a plain jerkin? It is even worse than that. This religious habit is a uniform for people who want to cause controversy and to warn their opponents that they should be ready to defend themselves. It can trigger a civil war in people's minds, and it would end up in fatal excesses if the king and his ministers were not as wise as the fanatics are irrational.

We know enough already about the costs incurred when Christians dispute about dogma. Blood has been spilled, both on scaffolds and in battles, from the fourth century to our own day. Let us limit ourselves here to the wars and horrors that resulted from disputes about the Reformation, and let us examine what were the sources of those misfortunes in France. A brief and accurate summary may possibly open the eyes of some people who are ignorant of that history, and may touch the hearts of those who have an open mind.

THREE

The Concept of Reformation in the Sixteenth Century

When minds began to be enlightened by the humanities during the Renaissance, there were also widespread complaints about abuses. Everyone agrees now that these complaints were justified.

Pope Alexander VI[1] had probably purchased his tiara, and his five bastard children shared the spoils of his office. His son, the Cardinal Duke of Borgia, together with his father the Pope, arranged the death of the Vitellis, the Urbinos, the Gravinas, the Oliverettos and the families of a hundred other noblemen in order to seize their lands. Julius II,[2] who was motivated by a similar ambition, excommunicated Louis XII and offered his kingdom to anyone who was willing to accept it while he himself, with a helmet on his head and a breastplate on his back, plundered part of Italy and killed its inhabitants. Pope Leo X,[3] in order to finance his luxuries, trafficked in indulgences as casually as merchants sell goods in a public market. Those who protested against this form of banditry were at least above moral reproach. Let us examine if they were equally justified when they objected to our political decisions.

The reformers said that since Jesus Christ had never looked for annates or reserved appointments,[4] nor had he sold pardons that applied in this life or indulgences that applied in the afterlife, there was no reason to pay the cost of all these items to a foreign prince. Although these annates, official requests to the Roman court and dispensations (which are still being sold today) would now cost us only 500,000 francs per annum, it is evident that since the time of Francis I – a period of 250 years – we have paid Rome 125 million francs. And if we take account of changes in the value of our currency, that would amount to approximately 250 million francs at today's prices. One may therefore agree, without fear of blasphemy, that when the heretics proposed to abolish these extraordinary taxes, which will shock our descendants, they did not thereby damage the kingdom and that we should think of them as good accountants rather than as disloyal subjects of the king. We should also add that they were the only ones who knew ancient Greek and they were well informed about antiquity. So we should not hide the fact that, despite their errors, we are indebted to them for enlightening human minds, which had been enslaved for a long period in the most impenetrable barbarism.

But since they also denied the reality of Purgatory, which we should not doubt (although it was very beneficial to the monks), and since they failed to revere relics that ought to be revered (although they were even more profitable) and eventually challenged some very highly respected dogmas,* the initial

* The reformers repeated the opinion of Berengarius about the Eucharist. They denied that a body was capable of being present simultaneously in 100,000 places, even by divine omnipotence; they denied that the attributes of a body could be present without the corresponding subject; they believed it was absolutely impossible for something that appeared as bread and wine to our eyes, our taste and our stomach to have been annihilated when these observable properties still exist; they defended all these errors, which had been condemned a long time ago in the case of Berengarius. They based their opinion on several passages written by the early Fathers of the Church, especially St Justin Martyr, who says explicitly in his *Dialogue with Trypho*: 'The offering of the consecrated bread is a symbol of the Eucharist that Jesus Christ commands us to celebrate in memory of his Passion.'

They recalled everything that was said during the first centuries of Christianity against the cult of relics. They quoted these words of Vigilantius: 'Is it necessary for you to revere or even adore vile dust? Do the souls of martyrs continue to animate their ashes? The customs of idolators are being introduced into the Church. They are beginning to light candles in the middle of the day. We may pray for each other while we are still alive, but what is the point of such prayers once we are dead?'

But they failed to say how much St Jerome objected to this passage. They wished to return completely to apostolic times and did not want to acknowledge that, as the Church expanded and gained power, it had to extend and

response was to burn them at the stake. The king, who protected and bribed them in Germany, marched at the head of a procession in Paris, after which some of these unfortunate people were executed. This is how they performed the execution. They suspended their victims at the end of a long wooden beam, which they then moved up and down like a seesaw that was balanced on a vertical shaft; they lit a great fire underneath them, and alternated between lowering them into the fire and lifting them up again. They were slowly tortured to death, until they eventually died by the most appalling and slowest method of execution that has ever been devised in the name of barbarity.

A short time before the death of Francis I, some members of the Provence *parlement*, who had been provoked by priests against the residents of Mérindol and Cabrières,[5] asked the king to send troops to assist in the execution of nineteen local people who had been condemned by them. They cut the throats of 6,000 villagers, without sparing women, old people or children and they reduced thirty villages to ashes. Those people who had lived in obscurity up to that time certainly made the mistake of being born as Waldensians;[6] that was their only crime. They had settled there more than 300 years earlier in barren and mountainous lands, which they had made fertile by incredible hard work. Their pastoral and idyllic lifestyle revived the innocence that characterized the early ages of mankind. They knew people in the neighbouring villages only because they visited them to sell their produce, and they knew nothing about legal disputes or wars. They never defended

---

fortify its religious practices. They condemned riches, which seemed nonetheless to have been necessary to support the magnificence of religious worship. [*Ed*. Berengarius of Tours (*c.* 999–1088) was classified as a heretic because he rejected the theology of transubstantiation. St Justin Martyr (*c.* 100–*c.* 165) was an early Christian apologist, whose *Dialogue with Trypho* includes an attempt to show the compatibility of Judaism and Christianity. St Jerome (347–420) was famous for his Latin translation of the Bible, known as the Vulgate.]

themselves and were executed as if they were animals trying to escape from a pen.*

Following the death of Francis I – a prince who was more famous for his gallantry and misfortunes than for cruelty – the execution of numerous heretics, especially that of Dubourg,[7] who was a counsellor at the *parlement*, and the massacre at Wassy,[8] provoked those who were persecuted to take up arms. Their numbers increased in proportion to the swords of executioners and the frequency with which people were burned at the stake. Patience was replaced by outrage. Those who

---

* The truthful and respected President de Thou wrote about these unfortunate, innocent people as follows: 'They were people who, about 300 years previously, had accepted rocky, uncultivated lands from their princes and, with extraordinary work and assiduous cultivation, they turned them into fertile lands that were suitable for livestock. They were extremely patient and dedicated to their work; they abhorred legal disputes, were generous to those in need, and paid taxes to their princes and the payments due to their lords scrupulously and honestly. They dedicated themselves to the cult of God with assiduous prayers and the innocence of their conduct. They rarely visited other people's places of worship unless they were visiting their neighbours to sell merchandise or for similar commercial reasons. Whenever they went there, they did not visit statues of God or saints, nor did they light candles in front of statues or donate money as offerings. They did not ask priests to perform sacred rituals for themselves or their relatives. They did not make the sign of the cross in the customary way; when they prayed, they did not sprinkle themselves with holy water but raised their eyes to Heaven and asked for God's help. They did not go abroad on pilgrimages nor raise their hats before images of the cross on the public roads. They celebrated an alternative rite in the vernacular; they did not defer to bishops or pontiffs but selected one of their members to preside over their meetings and instruct them. This is what was reported to Francis, in February, etc.'

Madame de Cental, who owned some of the ravaged lands where nothing could be seen apart from the corpses of its inhabitants, appealed to Henry II for justice. The king referred her appeal to the Paris *parlement*. The advocate general, whose name was Guérin and who was principally responsible for the massacres, was the only one condemned to death. De Thou says that he paid the penalty for all the others who were guilty because he had no friends in the court. [*Ed.* Voltaire quoted the long passage from de Thou in Latin. Jacques-Auguste de Thou (1553–1617) was the author of *Historiarum sui Temporis, Libri XVIII* {Eighteen Books on the History of his Times} (Paris, 1604), which was banned by Rome's *Index of Forbidden Books* because of the author's support for toleration (*Index*, 1704 edn, p. 136). De Thou subsequently helped draft the Edict of Nantes in 1598.]

were persecuted imitated the cruelty of their enemies. Nine civil wars filled France with carnage. A peace that was more fatal than war produced the St Bartholomew's Day Massacre,[9] which was unprecedented in the annals of crime.

The Catholic League assassinated Henry III and Henry IV, the former by the hands of a Jacobin monk and the latter by a monster who had been a member of the Feuillants.[10] There are some people who claim that humanity, toleration and freedom of conscience are appalling things. But could anyone say, in good faith, that they would have produced calamities that are comparable to what resulted from their rejection?

FOUR

Is Toleration Dangerous and which Nations Permit It?

Some have said that if we were to extend a paternal forbearance to our errant neighbours who pray to God in bad French,[1] that would amount to arming them and that we would repeat the battles of Jarnac, Moncontour, Coutras, Dreux, Saint-Denis[2] and so on. I cannot evaluate that objection, because I am not a prophet. But I do not think that it is logical to argue as follows: 'These people rebelled when I harmed them; therefore, they will rebel again if I treat them well.'

I venture to assume the liberty of inviting those who are responsible for governing the kingdom and those who are destined for high office to examine carefully the following: should we really fear that kindness will provoke the same revolts as cruelty has done in the past? Is what happened in certain circumstances in the past bound to happen again if the circumstances have changed? Do opinions, customs and manners remain unchanged forever?

The Huguenots were undoubtedly as drunk with fanaticism and as steeped in blood as we were. But is the current generation as barbarous as their predecessors? The age in which we live; Reason (which has made great progress); good books and the gentleness of our society – have all these factors not influenced those who guide the thinking of these peoples? And have we ourselves not noticed that almost the whole of Europe has changed its appearance during the past fifty years or so?

The government of countries has been strengthened everywhere, while at the same time people's manners have become more gentle. The regular police, supported by extensive standing armies, prevent us from fearing a return to those anarchic times when Calvinist peasants fought Catholic peasants, who were recruited hastily between the sowing season and harvest time.

In a new age there are new concerns. It would be absurd today to penalize the Sorbonne because, in the past, it petitioned to have Joan of Arc burned at the stake, because it decided that Henry III had lost his right to reign or because it excommunicated and banished the great Henry IV.[3] We would certainly not seek out other institutions of the kingdom that committed similar excesses in times of madness. That would be not only unjust, but it would be as foolish as purging the whole population of Marseille today because they suffered from the plague in 1720.

Should we go as far as to sack Rome, as Charles V's troops did, because Pope Sixtus V, in 1585, granted an indulgence of nine years to every Frenchman who would take up arms against his sovereign?[4] Is it not enough to prevent Rome from ever engaging in such excesses in future?

The fury that is inspired by a dogmatic understanding and abuse of the Christian religion, when it is misunderstood, has spilled as much blood and caused as many disasters in Germany, England and even in Holland as in France. Today, however, religious differences cause no problems in these states. Jews, Catholics, Greek Orthodox Christians, Lutherans, Calvinists, Anabaptists, Socinians, Moravians and so many others live together peacefully in these countries and contribute equally to the welfare of society.

People in Holland no longer fear that a theological dispute about predestination, by someone like Gomar,* would result in an old man being beheaded. In London they no longer fear

---

* Francis Gomar was a Protestant theologian. He defended the thesis, against his colleague Arminius, that God had destined most human beings from all eternity to burn for ever in Hell. This infernal dogma was reinforced, as one would expect, by persecution. The Grand Pensionary Barneveldt, who took sides with Gomar's opponents, was beheaded at the age of seventy-two, on 13 May 1619 'for having caused so much grief in God's church.' [*Ed.* Francis Gomar (1563–1641) and Jacob Arminius (1560–1609) were the leading theologians in the dispute about predestination in the United Provinces at the Synod of Dort (1618–19). Johan van Oldenbarnevelt (1547–1619), who held the office of Grand Pensionary in the States of Holland, was one of the most

that quarrels between Presbyterians and Episcopalians about the liturgy or about wearing a surplice would spill a king's blood[5] on a scaffold.* In an Ireland that has been enriched and repopulated, one will never again see scenes like the following: Catholic citizens of that country sacrificing its Protestant citizens for two whole months, burying them alive, hanging mothers from gibbets with their daughters tied to their mothers' necks and watching them die together, slashing the wombs of pregnant women and pulling out infants that are not fully formed, and feeding them to pigs and dogs; putting a dagger in the hands of their garroted prisoners and guiding it into the breast of their wives, fathers, mothers and daughters, thereby imagining that they turned them into mutual parricides and condemning them all to Hell in the process of exterminating them. That is what was reported by Rapin-Thoiras,[6] who served as an officer in Ireland at about the same time as these events occurred. That is what all the annals and histories of

---

powerful figures in Dutch political life and supported the more tolerant Arminian side in the dispute.]

* A declamation which defended the revocation of the Edict of Nantes says the following about England: 'A false religion inevitably produces such fruits, only one of which ripens; these insular people harvest it, and are despised by all nations.' One must acknowledge that the author used the opportunity to say that the English were despicable and universally despised. It does not seem to me, however, if a nation displays its bravery and generosity and is victorious in every part of the world, that it is then appropriate to say that it is despicable and despised. This odd passage occurs in a chapter about intolerance; one would expect those who preach intolerance to write that way. This abominable book, which looks as if it had been written by the madman of Verberie, comes from someone who had nothing better to do. What genuine pastor would write in that manner? The rage of this book went as far as justifying the St Bartholomew Massacre. One would imagine that such a book, filled with such appalling paradoxes, should be read by everyone, at least because it is so strange. But it remains almost unknown. [*Ed.* Voltaire quotes from Jean Novi de Caveirac (1713–82), *Apologie de Louis XIV et de son Conseil . . . avec une Dissertation sur la journée de la S. Barthélemi* {A Defence of Louis XIV and his Council, with a Dissertation about St Bartholomew's Day} (1758). The 'madman' to whom Voltaire refers is Jacques Ringuet, who was hanged in 1762 for having preached mad sermons and whom Voltaire mentions in the *Dictionnaire philosophique portatif* in the article entitled 'Supplices' {'Torture'}.]

England report, and it is something that undoubtedly will never happen again. Philosophy – and only philosophy, the sister of religion – has disarmed the hands of mankind that have been steeped in blood for such a long time by superstition. The human spirit, waking from its intoxication, is astonished at the excesses to which fanaticism has led it.

We ourselves in France have a prosperous province in which Lutherans are more numerous than Catholics. The University of Alsace is controlled by Lutherans, who also hold some of the municipal offices there. The province has never been disturbed by the slightest religious quarrel since it began to be ruled by our kings.[7] Why? Because no one was persecuted there. Do not try to interfere with people and you will win their loyalty.

I am not suggesting that all those who belong to churches other than that of the reigning prince should have the same access to honours and offices as those who believe in the religion of the majority. In England they suspect Catholics of supporting the Pretender[8] and they are denied access to public offices.[9] They even pay double tax, but they still enjoy all the rights of a citizen.

Some French bishops have been suspected of thinking that it is incompatible with their honour or best interests to have Calvinists in their diocese, and it is assumed that their concerns are the greatest obstacle to toleration. But I cannot believe that. The French episcopate includes highly qualified men who think and act with a nobility that reflects their ancestry. We must accept that they are charitable and generous. They believe that those who leave their diocese will surely not lapse from their faith when they visit foreign countries, and that when they return their pastors can enlighten them by their teaching and persuade them by their example. It would redound to their honour to convert them; there would be no civil losses involved, and the number of diocesan members would increase in proportion to the number of citizens.

A bishop in Warmia in Poland employed an Anabaptist as a farmer and a Socinian[10] as a tax collector. He was advised to dismiss the first one, because he did not believe in the doctrine of consubstantiality, and to harass the other because he did not baptize his son until he was fifteen years old. The bishop replied that both employees would be damned eternally in the next life but that, in this life, he very much needed their services.

Let us move outside our own local region and examine what happens in the rest of the wide world. The Sultan governs twenty peoples of different religions who live together peacefully. There are 200,000 Greeks living safely in Constantinople; and the Mufti himself nominates and presents the Greek Orthodox patriarch to the Emperor; they also allow a Latin rite patriarch in the same city. The Sultan nominates Latin rite bishops for some of the Greek islands,* by using the following official formula: 'I command him to go to the island of Chios as the resident bishop, in accordance with their ancient custom and their vain ceremonies.' This empire is full of Jacobites, Nestorians and Monothelites; there are also members of the Coptic rite there, members of the Church of St John, Jews, Gebers and Banians.[11] Nevertheless, the annals of Turkey never mention any rebellion that was initiated by any of these religions.

If you go to India, Persia or Tartary you will notice the same toleration and the same peace. Peter the Great protected all the religious cults that flourished in his immense empire; commerce and agriculture thrived and, as a result, the political system never experienced any trouble.

The government of China adopted only the cult of Noah during 4,000 years of its history, which involved the simple adoration of one God. At the same time they tolerated the superstitions of Fo and a multitude of mandarins who would have been dangerous had they not been restrained by the wisdom of their laws.

---

* Consult Ricaut. [*Ed.* Paul Ricaut (1628–1700) was an English explorer and historian and the author of *The Present State of the Ottoman Empire* (London, 1668), which was translated into French in 1670, and *The Present State of the Greek and Armenian Churches* (London, 1679), which was also translated into French in 1692.]

It is true that the great emperor Yung-Chin, who was possibly the wisest and most magnanimous ruler that was ever in
China, expelled the Jesuits.[12] But that was not because he was
intolerant but, on the contrary, because the Jesuits were intolerant. They themselves report, in their book entitled *Edifying
and Interesting Letters*,[13] the words with which this good
prince addressed them: 'I know that your religion is intolerant.
I know what you have done in the Philippines and in Japan.
You deceived my father, but do not think that you can also
deceive me.' If one were to read the whole discourse that the
Emperor deigned to address to them, one would conclude that
he was the wisest and most compassionate of men. How could
he have retained at court the services of European natural philosophers who had already kidnapped a prince of the royal
family while pretending to demonstrate the use of thermom-
eters and æolipyles at the court? And what would this emperor
have said if he had read our histories and had known about the
times when we had the Catholic League and the Gunpowder
Plot?[14]

It was enough for him to have been informed about the dis-
gusting disputes between Jesuits, Dominicans, Capuchins and
secular priests who were sent into his empire from the other
ends of the world. They came there to preach the truth and
then accused each other of heresy. All the Emperor did was to
repatriate some foreign troublemakers. But how kind he was
to them as he sent them on their way! What paternal care he
took to arrange their journey and to guarantee that no one
insulted them as they left! Even their banishment was an
example of toleration and humanity.

The Japanese were the most tolerant of all people.* Twelve
peaceful religions were already established in their empire
when the Jesuits arrived to add a thirteenth.[15] But very soon

---

* Consult Kempfer and all the reports about Japan. [*Ed.* Engelbert Kämpfer
(1651–1716) was a German surgeon and explorer who wrote extensively
about Japan, including a *History of Japan*, which was published posthumously in 1727.]

after their arrival the Jesuits showed that they were unwilling to tolerate any other religion and we know what happened as a result. A civil war that was no less appalling than that of the Catholic League devastated the whole country. The Christian religion was drowned in a tide of blood. The Japanese closed their empire to the rest of the world and they thought of us as nothing better than wild animals that resembled those that the English had purged from their island. Minister Colbert,[16] who understood that we needed the Japanese while they did not need us, tried in vain to develop trade with their empire, but he found that they were adamant.

Thus our whole continent proves that we should neither promote nor practise intolerance.

Cast your eyes towards the other side of the world. Look at Carolina, where the wise John Locke drafted their legislation and where seven heads of families are enough to establish a religion that the law then approves.[17] This liberty does not cause any disorder. God forbid that we should cite this example as something that France should emulate! I report it here only to show that the greatest possible degree of toleration did not cause the least conflict, although what is very useful and beneficial in a nascent colony may not be appropriate in an ancient kingdom.

What should we say about those simple people who are derisively called Quakers and who, by practices that may be ridiculous, have been so virtuous and have taught peace to everyone else, although unsuccessfully? There are 100,000 Quakers in Pennsylvania; discord and controversy are unknown in the happy homeland that they established for themselves there, and even the name of their city of Philadelphia, which reminds them constantly of the brotherhood of mankind, is both an example and a reproach to peoples that have not yet discovered toleration.[18]

Finally, toleration has never provoked civil war, whereas intolerance has covered the earth in carnage. Let people now choose between these two rivals: between the mother who wants her son to be slain, and the mother who is willing to surrender him on condition that he survives.[19]

I am concerned here only with the interests of nations and, while respecting theology, as I ought, I consider in this essay only the physical and moral well-being of society. I implore every impartial reader to weigh up these truths and to correct and develop them. Attentive readers who share their thoughts with others will make more progress than the author.*

* M. de la Bourdonnaie, the Intendant of Rouen, says that the manufacture of hats has declined at Caudebec and Neufchâtel because so many refugees have departed. M. Foucaut, the Intendant of Caen, says that commercial activity has been reduced by half. M. de Maupeou, the Intendant of Poitiers, says that the production of druggets has collapsed completely. M. de Bezons, the Intendant of Bordeaux, complains that there is hardly any commercial activity at all in Clérac or Nérac. M. de Miroménil, the Intendant of Touraine, says that trade in Tours has decreased by ten million livres per annum. All these reductions result from religious persecution. Consult the *Mémoires* of 1698. Above all, count the number of officers on land and sea, and the number of sailors, who were forced to leave France and serve against their own country in foreign armies, often with fatal consequences, and then judge if intolerance has been detrimental to the State.

I do not have the temerity here to offer advice to ministers whose intelligence and good intentions are well known and whose loyalty is as noble as their ancestry; they will see clearly that in order to restore our navy we must exercise some degree of toleration towards the inhabitants of our coasts. [*Ed.* Henri de Boulainvilliers (1658–1722), *Mémoires présentés à Monseigneur le Duc D'Orléans, Régent de France* {Memoirs Presented to the Duke of Orleans, Regent of France}(The Hague, 1727), 2 vols., collected evidence to support the conclusion that France was weakened militarily and commercially by the emigration of Huguenots after the Edict of Nantes was revoked.]

FIVE

How to Accommodate Toleration

I venture to assume that an enlightened and magnanimous minister, a humanitarian and wise prelate, or a prince who realizes that his interests depend on having a large number of subjects and whose glory would be enhanced by their well-being, might deign to glance at this defective and unstructured essay. If he were to supplement it with his own insights, he might say to himself: 'What would I risk in order to see the land cultivated and improved by having many extra labourers, to see an increase in revenues and to see the State flourishing much more?'

Germany would be a desert covered with the skeletons of Catholics, Evangelicals, Reformers and Anabaptists who had massacred each other if the peace of Westphalia had not eventually secured freedom of conscience for its inhabitants.

We have Jews in Bordeaux, Metz and Alsace; we also have Lutherans, Molinists and Jansenists.[1] Could we not tolerate and accommodate Calvinists under approximately the same conditions as Catholics are tolerated in London? The more sects there are, the less dangerous each one of them becomes.[2] Their sheer number makes each one of them weaker. They are all restrained by just laws that prohibit large gatherings, insults and seditions, and which are effective as a result of public support for the law.

We know that many heads of families who have made fortunes in foreign countries are willing to return to their homeland. All they request is that they may enjoy the protection of natural law, that the validity of their marriages be recognized, that their children be protected by the State and have a right to inherit from their fathers and that their personal safety be guaranteed. They are not asking for public buildings for religious worship, a right to public funds or that they be conferred with honours. Catholics do not enjoy any such rights in London or in many other countries. There is no longer a question of granting them major privileges or designating secure places for a particular sect;[3] it is only a matter of allowing a peaceful people to survive and of relaxing certain edicts that may have been necessary in the past but are no longer so. It is not up to me to tell the minister what he can do; it is enough for us to implore him on behalf of these unfortunate people.[4]

There are so many ways to make the Huguenots useful and to make sure that they are never dangerous. The prudence of the minister and the Council, when supported by the police, will very easily identify measures that so many other nations already use.

There are still fanatics within the Calvinist population, but it is true that there are even more among enthusiasts in the wider population. The nation pays no attention to the insane human dregs of Saint-Médard, but those who survive as prophets among the Calvinists are annihilated.[5] If there are still some maniacs among us, the best way to reduce their number is to assign this mental illness to the control of reason, which slowly but infallibly enlightens mankind. Reason is gentle and humane, and it encourages toleration; it eliminates discord, reinforces virtue and is more effective in persuading people to obey the law than force is in winning their compliance. One should also not underestimate the ridicule with which all sensible people regard religious enthusiasm in our time. This ridicule is a powerful barrier against the excesses of all religious sects. The past may be regarded as if it never occurred; one must begin again from the present moment in which we live and from the progress that peoples have made to date.

There was a time when it was considered necessary to issue legal prohibitions against those who taught any doctrine contrary to Aristotle's categories, nature's abhorrence of a vacuum, quiddities, or to universals as being parts of the individuals in which they are exemplified.[6] In Europe we have more than a hundred volumes of laws about sorcery and how to distinguish between genuine sorcery and its imitations.[7] It was once very common to excommunicate locusts and other insects that damage crops, which is still practised in some religious rituals today.[8] Customs also change; we now leave Aristotle, sorcerers and locusts unmolested. There are countless examples of these serious insanities, which were once very important; others are revived from time to time, but once people see their effects and have had enough of them, they self-destruct. If anyone in our day thought of becoming a Carpocratian, a Eutychian, a Monothelite, a Monophysite, a Nestorian or a Manichaean,[9] etc., what would happen to them? People would simply laugh at them, as if they had dressed up in ancient clothes with a doublet and ruff.

Our nation began to open its eyes when two Jesuits, Le Tellier and Doucin, concocted the papal bull *Unigenitus* and sent it to Rome.[10] They thought they were still living in those ignorant times when people believed everything they were told, no matter how absurd it was. They even dared to condemn the following proposition, which is universally true in all circumstances and at all times: 'Fear of an unjust excommunication should never prevent someone from doing their duty.' That was equivalent to proscribing reason, the liberties of the Gallican Church and the very foundation of morality. It was as if they said to people: God commands you not to do your duty any time you fear that injustice may result. Common sense has never been so affronted. The Pope's advisers in Rome failed to realize the implications of their decision. They were convinced in the Roman curia that this bull was necessary and that the French nation had requested it. The bull was signed, sealed and officially promulgated. We now know its consequences.[11] If they had anticipated these effects, they would certainly have amended the bull. It provoked acrimonious disputes, which were resolved only by the prudence and goodwill of the king.

The same applies to many of the disputed doctrines that separate us from Protestants. Some of these are trivial, while others are more important, but even in the latter cases the

passion of the disputes has abated so much that even Protestants no longer preach the opposite doctrine in any of their
churches.

We should therefore welcome this age of disgust and satiety
or rather of Reason, as one in which we commit ourselves to
public harmony. Religious controversy is an epidemic that has
run its course and this plague, of which we have been cured,
no longer needs anything more than a mild diet. The interest
of the State demands that exiled sons be allowed to return to
their fathers' homes without fanfare; human decency requires
that we allow them, reason advises it, and public policy has no
reason to fear it.

SIX

Does Natural or Civil Law Permit Intolerance?

Natural law is that which nature reveals to all human beings. Thus, when you have reared a child, the child owes you respect as their father and recognition as their benefactor. You have a right to the produce of land that you have cultivated with your own labour. When you make a promise or when someone else makes a promise to you, it must be honoured.

Civil laws about specific issues must be founded on natural law. The great principle – the universal principle of both laws that applies throughout the land – is as follows: 'Do not do what you would not like someone to do to you.' Now, according to this principle, it would be impossible for one person to say to another: 'Believe what I believe and what you cannot believe, or you will die.' That is what they say in Portugal, Spain and Goa. In some countries today they only go so far as to say: 'Either believe or I shall shun you; believe or I shall harm you as much as I possibly can. You are a monster and since you do not profess the same religion as I do, you therefore have none at all. You must be shunned by your neighbours, your village and your province.'

If civil law approved such conduct, then the Japanese would have to detest the Chinese, who in turn would loathe the people of Siam. They in turn would then detest those who live by the Ganges, who would hate those who live by the Indus River. Mongolians would massacre the first resident of the Malabar region[1] that they met, and the Malabarians would kill Persians, who in turn would kill Turks. And all of them together would attack Christians, who have been devouring each other for such a long time.

The law of intolerance is therefore absurd and barbaric. It is the law of the jungle and, indeed, it is even worse because wild animals kill others only to eat, while we human beings are exterminating each other for the sake of a few paragraphs.

SEVEN

Was Intolerance Known among the Greeks?

The various peoples about whom history has provided some meagre information have all perceived their different religions as ties that bound them together in a shared humanity. Their gods had a certain right to hospitality, just like human beings. Thus, when strangers arrived in a town, they began by worshipping the local gods. One never failed to venerate even the enemy's gods. The Trojans prayed to the gods who were fighting on behalf of the Greeks.[1]

Alexander the Great went out into the Libyan desert to consult the god Amun-Ra, whom the Greeks called Zeus and the Romans called Jupiter, although both had their own Zeus and Jupiter in their own lands. When they laid siege to a town, they offered a sacrifice and prayers to the gods of that town to achieve a favourable outcome. Thus, even in the thick of battle, religion was a unifying factor among men, and it sometimes mitigated their ferocity, even though it commanded them at other times to commit the most appallingly inhumane acts.

I may be mistaken about this, but it seems to me that among all the civilized peoples of the ancient world none of them ever obstructed freedom of thought. They all had some religion, but they seem to have practised it among human beings in the same way as they did in relation to the gods; they all recognized a supreme god, with which they associated a prodigious number of lower deities. Likewise, they had only one general cult, but they allowed people to practise it in a wide range of alternative ways.

The Greeks, for example, despite the fact that they were religious, found it acceptable for Epicureans to deny providence and the existence of the human soul. I shall say nothing about the other sects in Greece, all of which offended the rational ideas that one ought to have about the existence of the Creator and all of which were nonetheless tolerated.

Socrates, who came closer than anyone else to knowing the Creator, paid the price (as we say) for his discovery and died as a martyr for the Divinity. He was the only one whom the Greeks killed because of the opinions that he held. If that really was the reason for his condemnation, it would not in any way support intolerance, because they punished the only person who glorified God, while they honoured all those who applied the most unworthy concepts to the Divinity. The enemies of toleration, in my opinion, should not appeal to the odious example of those who judged Socrates as if it provided evidence to support their view.

It is obvious, moreover, that Socrates was the victim of a hostile mob that conspired against him. He made irreconcilable enemies of the sophists, orators and poets who taught in the schools and even of all the teachers who were responsible for educating the children of prominent families. He himself admitted, in the speech that was reported in Plato's dialogue, that he used to go from house to house to demonstrate to those teachers that they were simply ignorant.[2] That kind of conduct was inappropriate for someone who had been described by an oracle as the wisest of men. A priest and a member of the Council of Five Hundred were so provoked that they lodged an accusation against him. I must acknowledge that I do not know the precise terms of the accusation, since I find that his *Apology* is rather vague about it. In general terms, he was said to have incited young people with ideas that were dangerous to religion and to the government of the nation. That is how calumniators always operate, all over the world. But, in a court of law, one must have facts that are confirmed by witnesses and an indictment that provides detailed and precise charges. That is what we fail to find in the trial of Socrates. All we know is that he initially had 220 votes in his favour. The jury therefore included 220 philosophers, which is a considerable number, and I doubt if one would find that many elsewhere. The majority, however, decided that he should take the hemlock. But we should also remember that, when the Athenians came to their senses, they loathed the prosecutors. Meletus, who was the leader of those who supported the verdict, was condemned to death because it was unjust and the other judges were banished into exile, but a temple was built in memory of Socrates. Philosophy has never been vindicated as well or honoured as much. The example of Socrates is ultimately the most convincing argument that can be made against intolerance. The Athenians had an altar dedicated to foreign gods – to gods that they were unable to know. Is there any greater proof, not only of tolerating all nations, but also of respecting their cults?

A decent gentleman[3] – someone who was not an enemy of reason, literature or of probity and who served his nation well – was recently justifying the St Bartholomew's Day Massacre by comparing it with the Phocian war (the so-called 'holy war') as if that war had been waged for religious reasons, for the sake of dogma or because of theological disputes. In fact, it arose because of a dispute about the ownership of a piece of land, which is the reason why all wars are fought. Sheaves of wheat do not constitute a confession of faith. No Greek city ever went to war because of disputes about what people believed. What exactly, then, is this modest and kind man proposing? Would he want us to wage another holy war?

EIGHT

Were the Romans Tolerant?

Among the ancient Romans, from Romulus to the time when Christians disputed with the priests of the Roman Empire, you do not find a single person who was persecuted because of their beliefs. Cicero was sceptical about everything and Lucretius denied everything; yet neither of them experienced the slightest reproach. Citizens enjoyed so much freedom that Pliny the naturalist began his book by denying God and saying that if there is a god it is the Sun.[1] Cicero wrote, when speaking about Hell: *Non est anus tam excors quae credat*; 'There is no old woman who is foolish enough to believe that.'[2] Juvenal wrote: *Nec pueri credunt*; 'Even children do not believe it.'[3] They used to chant in the Roman theatre:

> There is nothing after death,
> Death itself is nothing.[4]

We should abhor those sentiments, but we should also excuse them because those who expressed them were not enlightened by the Gospels. They are false and impious opinions. But we should also conclude that the Romans were very tolerant, because those same views never provoked them to raise the slightest objection.

The great principle that was adopted by the Roman senate and people was: *Deorum offensae diis curae*, that is, the gods alone should be concerned about offences against the gods. This royal people thought only of conquering, governing and civilizing the universe. They were our legislators as much as our conquerors. Caesar, who gave us swords, laws and public entertainments, never wanted us to abandon our Druids and change our allegiance to him, despite the fact that he was the great pontiff of the nation that ruled us.

The Romans did not profess all religions and did not approve of them all publicly, but they did allow all of them to be practised. Under the reign of Numa Pompilius,[5] they did not use any material objects in their religious rites – there were no images of gods or statues. Soon after that, however, they erected images of some gods of the principal nations in the Empire, to which the Greeks had introduced them. The Law of the Twelve Tables[6] – which required them not to revere foreign gods – implied nothing more than limiting public homage to those gods that were approved by the senate. Isis had a temple in Rome until Tiberius demolished it, after priests of that temple, corrupted by bribes from Mundus, allowed him to impersonate the god Anubis and to sleep in the temple with a woman called Paulina. It is true that Josephus was the only one who reported this story;[7] besides, he was not a contemporary, and he was credulous and likely to exaggerate. It is unlikely that, in a period as enlightened as that of Tiberius, a woman from a prominent family could have been foolish enough to believe that she had won the favour of the god Anubis.

But whether this anecdote is true or false it is still certain that Egyptian superstition built a temple in Rome with the support of the public. The Jews were engaged in business there since the time of the Punic wars and they had synagogues there since the time of Augustus, which they have maintained almost without interruption until now. Is there any better demonstration that the Romans considered toleration to be the most sacred of civil laws?

Some may object that once Christians arrived they were persecuted by these same Romans who (allegedly) never persecuted anyone. It seems to me that this claim is completely false. I need only St Paul himself to prove it. The Acts of the Apostles tell us* that when the Jews accused St Paul of attempting to destroy Mosaic law by substituting Jesus Christ in its place, St James advised him to shave his head and go to the temple to purify himself, 'so that everyone will know that everything

---

* Acts 21, 22.

they say about you is false and that you continue to observe the law of Moses'.[8]

Paul, a Christian, then began to observe the Jewish rituals for seven days. But before the seven days had expired some Jews from Asia recognized him and, when they saw that he had entered the temple and was accompanied not only by Jews but also by Gentiles, they protested about its profanation. Paul was arrested, brought before the governor Felix and subsequently before the tribunal of Festus. A crowd of Jews demanded his death. Festus replied to them:* 'It is not customary for Romans to condemn a man before the accused has been confronted by his accusers and has had an opportunity to defend himself.'

These words by this Roman magistrate were all the more remarkable because he seems to have had no respect for St Paul and to have treated him with contempt. Since he was misguided by the false light of his own reason, he took him for a fool. He said to himself that he was a lunatic:† 'Much learning has made you mad.' The equity of Roman law, therefore, was alone sufficient to persuade Festus to provide protection for an unknown person for whom he had no respect.

The Holy Spirit thus declares, in this text, that the Romans were not persecutors and that they were just. It was not the Romans who attacked St Paul, but the Jews. St James, the brother of Jesus, was stoned to death on the orders of a Saducean Jew rather than those of a Roman. It was only the Jews who stoned St Stephen;‡ and when St Paul was minding the cloaks of his executioners, he was certainly not acting as a Roman citizen.[9]

The first Christians were almost certainly not involved in any controversy with the Romans; their only enemies were the Jews,

---

* Acts 25.

† Acts 26:34 [*Ed*. The correct reference in Acts 26:24].

‡ Although the Jews did not have a right to hear criminal cases since Archelaus was exiled among the Allobroges, and Judea was governed as a province in the Roman Empire, the Romans nonetheless turned a blind eye when the Jews applied their zeal to judging someone, that is, when they stoned to death in a sudden outburst someone whom they believed was guilty of blasphemy. [*Ed*. Archelaus (23 BC–AD 18), the son of Herod the Great, was banished to Vienne, in south-eastern Gaul, in AD 6.]

from whom they wanted to separate. It is well known how much members of any sect hate those who leave their sect. There was undoubtedly an uproar in the synagogues of Rome. Suetonius writes, in his life of Claudius: 'He expelled the Jews from Rome because they were constantly disturbing the peace in the name of Christ.'[10] He was mistaken in claiming that it was instigated by Christ. He could not have been adequately informed about a people who were as despised as the Jews were in Rome, but he was not mistaken about the reason for the disputes. Suetonius was writing during the reign of Hadrian, in the second century, when the Romans had not yet distinguished between Christians and Jews. The quotation from Suetonius shows that the Romans, far from oppressing the early Christians, repressed the Jews who persecuted them. They wanted the synagogue in Rome to exercise as much toleration towards their separated Christian brethren as the Roman senate had shown to the Jews, who soon returned after they had been expelled. They even conferred honours on them, despite the fact that the law forbade that practice. We know this on the authority of Dio Cassius[11] and Ulpian.* Is it possible that, after the destruction of Jerusalem, the emperors showered the Jews with honours but persecuted Christians – whom they identified as a sect of Jews – by throwing them to the lions and executioners?

We are told that Nero persecuted the Christians. Tacitus tells us that they were accused of setting fire to Rome and that they were then abandoned to the anger of the people. Has that accusation anything to do with their beliefs? Certainly not. Would we say that the Chinese who were slaughtered by the Dutch a few years ago in the suburbs of Batavia were sacrificed for their religion?[12] No matter how much we might wish to deceive ourselves, it is impossible to claim that intolerance was responsible for the disaster that befell a few unfortunate half-Jews and half-Christians during Nero's reign.†

---

* Ulpian, *Digest* I, ii: 'Those who followed the Jewish superstition were allowed to acquire honours.' [*Ed*. The full reference is Book L, Title II, iii.]
† Tacitus writes: 'The common people called those who were invisible because of their shameful behaviour Christians.'

It is rather difficult to believe that the name 'Christian' was already being used in Rome at that time. Tacitus wrote during the reign of Vespasian and Domitian. He wrote about Christians in the same way as people spoke about them at the time. I would venture to say that the words '*odio humani generis convicti*', as used by Tacitus, could have meant 'convicted by the hatred of the human race' just as easily as 'convicted of hating the human race'.

What, in fact, did these first missionaries do in Rome? They tried to win some souls and taught them the purest morality. They did not rebel against any powers. The humility of their hearts corresponded with that of their status and condition. They were almost unknown and were scarcely distinguished from Jews. How could people who did not know them have hated them, and how could they have been convicted of detesting such people?

When London burned, Catholics were accused. But the fire occurred after the wars of religion and after the Gunpowder Plot for which several disgraceful Catholics were convicted.

The first Christians, who lived during the reign of Nero, certainly did not find themselves in similar circumstances. It is very difficult to see through the clouds of history. Tacitus provides no evidence to suspect that Nero himself wanted to reduce Rome to ashes. One would have more reason to suspect that Charles II set fire to London! The blood of his father the king, who had been executed on a public scaffold in front of people who were calling for his death, would at least have provided an excuse for Charles II. But Nero had no excuse, no pretext and no interest in setting fire to Rome. These silly rumours circulate among people in every country; we have heard rumours that are just as foolish and unjust in our own day.

Tacitus, who was well acquainted with the way in which princes tend to behave, should also have known about the character of the people, which is always vain, always extravagant in its violent and fickle opinions, incapable of understanding anything properly and which is capable of saying anything, believing anything and forgetting everything.

Philo says that 'Seianus persecuted them during the reign of Tiberius, but after the death of Seianus the Emperor restored all their rights.' They had the same rights as Roman citizens, despite the fact that the Roman citizens despised them. They shared in the wheat harvest, although, when the distribution coincided with the Sabbath, they deferred their share to another day. That was probably due to the monies they paid the State, because they purchased toleration in every country and were quickly compensated for the costs they incurred in doing so.

This passage from Philo explains perfectly the other passage from Tacitus, which says that four thousand Jews or Egyptians were sent to Sardinia, and if the harsh climate there caused them to perish, that was a small loss or, in Latin, a '*vile damnum*'.

I shall add to this comment that Philo thought of Tiberius as a wise and just ruler. I am sure he was just only insofar as justice coincided with his own interests. But the good things that Philo reports about him make me a little doubtful about the horrors of which Tacitus and Suetonius accuse him. I do not think it was likely that an infirm old man, at the age of seventy, retired to the Isle of Capri to devote himself to strange debaucheries that are hardly natural and were even unknown to the most libertine young people of Rome. Neither Tacitus nor Suetonius knew this emperor; they just enjoyed collecting popular rumours. Octavius, Tiberius and their successors were odious because they dominated a people that should have been free. Historians delight in defaming them, and these histories were believed without supporting evidence because they had no contemporary records, documents or news publications. Besides, these historians do not quote anyone, and therefore one cannot contradict them. They defame anyone they wish and determine arbitrarily the judgement of posterity. Wise readers should distrust the veracity of these historians and decide to what extent they should believe public events that are reported by serious authors who are born in an enlightened nation, and what limits they should set for their own credulity about anecdotes that such authors report without any supporting evidence. [*Ed.* The first two Tacitus quotations are from his *Annals*, 15.44. Vespasian (9–79) and Domitian (51–96) were Roman emperors, respectively, in 69–79 and 81–96. The Great Fire of London occurred in 1666. Lucius Aelius Seianus (20 BC–AD 31), known as Sejanus, served under Tiberius. The passage from Tacitus about the 4,000 Jews or Egyptians is taken from *Annals*, II, 85.]

NINE

Martyrs

During the following centuries there were Christian martyrs. It is very difficult to discover why exactly these martyrs were condemned to death, but I venture to suggest that during the reign of the first Caesars not one of them was condemned exclusively because of their religion. All religions were tolerated in the Empire. How then could they have selected and persecuted some obscure people who belonged to one particular sect during a period when all other sects were tolerated?

Emperors such as Titus, Trajan, Antoninus and Decius were not barbarians. Is it possible to imagine that they would have deprived only Christians of a freedom that everyone else enjoyed? Is it possible that only Christians could have been accused of being involved in secret mysteries, when those of Isis, of Mithras and of the goddess of Assyria – all of which were foreign to the Roman cult – were allowed without any objection? There must have been other reasons for persecuting Christians; particular instances of hatred, supported by political reasons, must have been responsible for shedding the blood of Christians.

For example, when St Lawrence refused to hand over to the prefect of Rome, Cornelius Secularius, the Christians' money that he was guarding, it was natural for the prefect and the Emperor to become angry. They did not know that St Lawrence distributed this money to the poor, and that he was engaged in charitable and holy work. They thought of him simply as someone who refused to obey orders and put him to death.*

---

* We certainly respect everything that the Church requires us to respect. We invoke the intercession of martyred saints, but, while revering St Lawrence, is it

Let us consider the martyrdom of St Polyeuctus.[1] Was he condemned only because of his religion? He went into the temple, when they were giving thanks to the gods for the victory of the emperor Decius. He insulted those who were offering sacrifices, and he overturned and broke the altars and the statues. Is there any country in the world where they would forgive such an attack? The Christian who publicly tore up the decree of the emperor Diocletian and thereby provoked the great persecution of his religious brethren in the final two years of the ruler's reign was not zealous in the proper sense, and was very unfortunate to have caused the disaster that befell his sect.[2] This misguided zeal, which often erupted and was even condemned by many Church Fathers, was probably the source of all those persecutions.

I certainly do not intend to compare the Sacramentarians[3] with the first Christians; I do not put error and truth side by side. But Farel,[4] who was the predecessor of Jean Calvin, did exactly the same thing in Arles as St Polyeuctus had done in Armenia. People were walking in a procession in the streets and were carrying a statue of St Anthony the Hermit.[5] Farel and some of his associates attacked the monks who were carrying St Anthony; they beat them and chased them away and then threw St Anthony into the river. Farel would have deserved the death penalty, which he avoided only because he had time to escape. If he had been satisfied only to shout at

---

not possible to doubt the story that St Sixtus said to him: 'You will follow me within three days'? May we not doubt that, within that short interval of time, the prefect commanded him to surrender the Christians' money, that the deacon Lawrence had time to assemble all the poor people in the town, that he travelled to the prefect to lead him to the place where the poor were assembled; that the trial took place there and that he was interrogated; that the prefect commanded a blacksmith to construct a grill that was sufficiently large to roast a man on it; that the first magistrate of Rome assisted in person in such a strange execution; that St Lawrence said, while he was on the grill: 'I am cooked well enough on this side, so turn me over to the other side if you want to eat me.' Such a grill is hardly consistent with the character of the Romans. And how did it happen that no pagan author has ever mentioned a similar strange event? [*Ed.* St Lawrence was a deacon during the papacy of Sixtus II and was believed to have been burned alive on a gridiron within days of the Pope's execution under Valerian in 258. The legend about St Lawrence is reported in St Ambrose, *De Officiis*, I, 41.]

those monks that he did not believe the story about a crow
bringing half a loaf to St Anthony the hermit, or the legend
that St Anthony had engaged in conversations with centaurs
and satyrs, he would have deserved only a formal reprimand
for having caused a breach of the peace. But if, instead, when
the procession had finished that evening, he had examined
peacefully the story about the crow or about the centaurs and
satyrs, there would have been no reason to reproach him at all.

But is it possible that the Romans would have allowed the
infamous Antinous[6] to be ranked among the secondary gods
and, at the same time, that they would have torn apart and
thrown to the lions all those who could have been accused of
nothing more serious than adoring the true God in a peaceful
manner? That they would have recognized a supreme God,* a
sovereign God who is superior to all celestial beings, is

---

* One only has to open Virgil to see that the Romans recognized a supreme
God, who is sovereign over all celestial beings.

> O Jupiter, who rules the affairs of men and gods
>   with eternal laws, and threatens them with thunder.
> O father, O eternal power of men and gods.

Horace expresses himself much more vigorously:

> Nothing greater than himself originates from him,
> Nor is there anything like him or even close to him.

The Romans chanted nothing other than the unity of God in the mysteries
into which they were nearly all initiated. Consider the wonderful hymn of
Orpheus; read the letter that Maximus of Madaura wrote to St Augustine, in
which he wrote that 'only fools could fail to recognize a sovereign God.'
Longinianus was a pagan, and wrote to St Augustine that God 'is unique,
incomprehensible, ineffable'. Even Lactantius, who could hardly have been
accused of being too tolerant, admits (in Book V) that the Romans made all
the gods subject to the supreme God: 'He subjected them and handed them
over to God.' Even Tertullian, in his *Apologetics*, concedes that the whole
Empire acknowledged a God who was master of the universe, whose power
and majesty were infinite, 'ruler of the world, with perfect power and majesty'. Above all, consult Plato, who was Cicero's teacher in philosophy, and
you will see 'that there is only one God who must be adored and loved, and
whom one must try to resemble in holiness and justice'. Epictetus in irons,
Marcus Antoninus on his heavenly throne, say the same thing a hundred times.
[*Ed.* The quotations from Virgil's *Aeneid* are from I, 229–30, and X, 18. The

confirmed by this expression: 'the greatest and best God', and they would have pursued those who adored a unique God.

It is not credible that, under the Roman emperors, there ever was an Inquisition against Christians, if that meant they were interrogated about their religious beliefs. They did not bother Jews, Syrians, Egyptians, poets, druids or philosophers about their beliefs. The martyrs, therefore, were those who opposed false gods. It was very wise and dutiful on their part not to believe in them, but if they were not content to worship God in spirit and in truth and if instead they clashed violently with the established cult – however absurd it may have been – one must conclude that they were the ones who were intolerant.

Tertullian in his *Apologetics* admits that Christians were regarded as seditious.* The accusation is unjust, but it demonstrates that it was not simply the religion of Christians that provoked the zeal of magistrates. He admits that the Christians refused to decorate their doors with laurel branches during

---

third line is given in modern editions of the Latin text as 'power of men and things'. The Horace quotation is from *Odes*, I, 18. The Orphic hymns were a collection of short religious poems composed in either the late Hellenistic (3rd or 2nd century BC) or early Roman (1st to 2nd century AD) era, which were thought to reflect the teachings of the mythical hero Orpheus. Maximus of Madaura wrote to St Augustine, Letter 16 in the standard edition of Augustine's correspondence. The citation from Lactantius is found in *Divine Institutes* (Book V, 3), trans. A. Bowen and P. Garnsey (Liverpool: Liverpool University Press, 2003), p. 289. The reference to Tertullian is from his *Apologetics*, 24, 3. The moral ideal of resembling god (*homoiōsis theōi*) was prominent in traditional readings of Plato, and was based on the *Theaetetus* 176B ('to become like god is to become just and holy') and on the *Republic* 613A–B (to be just is 'to become as like god as is possible').]

* Chapter 39 [*Ed.* In this chapter the early Christian theologian Tertullian (*c.* 160–*c.* 240) rejects the perception of Christians as seditious or a danger to the state. 'But who has ever suffered harm from our assemblies? We are in our congregations just what we are when separated from each other; we are as a community what we are as individuals; we injure nobody, we trouble nobody. When the upright, when the virtuous meet together, when the pious, when the pure assemble in congregation, you ought not to call that a faction, but a curia – i.e., the court of God.']

public celebrations of the emperors' victories.* This reprehensible affectation would have been understood as a treasonable
crime.

The reign of Domitian was the first time that Christians
were subjected to severe penalties, but they were limited to
exile that lasted less than a year. 'He quickly rescinded his
orders and readmitted those whom he had banished,' says
Tertullian.[7] Lactantius, who tends to exaggerate things, agrees
that the Church was peaceful and flourishing from the time of
Domitian to that of Decius.† The long peace, he says, was
interrupted when that detestable animal, Decius, oppressed
the Church. 'After many years, the detestable animal Decius
came along and persecuted the Church.'[8]

I do not wish to discuss the opinion of the learned Mr Dodwell[9] about how few martyrs there were. But if the Romans
had persecuted the Christian religion as much as was claimed,
if they had plunged Christians into boiling oil and had exposed
completely naked girls to lions in the circus, how could they
have left unmolested all the first bishops of Rome? St Irenaeus
included only one of those bishops, Telesphorus, among the
martyrs in the year 139 and there was no proof that this Telesphorus was put to death.[10] Zephyrinus[11] governed the flock of
Rome for eighteen years and died peacefully in 219. It is true
that almost all the early popes were included in the old martyrologies, but the word 'martyr' was used in its proper sense in
those days. The word 'martyr' means 'witness' rather than
'torture' or 'execution'.

It is difficult to reconcile the reported intensity of persecutions with the freedom with which Christians assembled in
fifty-six councils, which ecclesiastical writers report took place
in the first three centuries.

There were indeed persecutions, but if they had been as violent as we were told, it is probable that Tertullian, who wrote

* Chapter 35 [Ed. 'Why, on the day of gladness, do we neither cover our
door-posts with laurels, nor intrude upon the day with lamps? Is it a proper
thing, at the call of a public festivity, to dress your house up like some new
brothel?']

† Chapter 3 [Ed. De mortibus persecutorum {On the Deaths of Persecutors.]

so trenchantly against the established cult, would not have died in his bed. It is well known that the emperors did not read his *Apologetics*, that such an obscure book, written in Africa, did not reach those who were responsible for governing the world in Rome. But those who were close to the proconsul of Africa should have known about it; it ought to have provoked much hatred of the author and yet he did not suffer martyrdom.

Origen taught publicly in Alexandria and was not put to death. This same Origen, who spoke with so much freedom to pagans and Christians – telling one group about Jesus and denying a Trinitarian God to the others – explicitly concedes in his third book against Celsus that 'there were very few martyrs and long intervals between them. Nonetheless (he writes) Christians lost no opportunity to have everyone adopt their religion. They spread throughout the cities, towns and villages.'[12]

It is certain that priests of a different sect could easily have interpreted these frequent journeys as seditious, but these missions were still tolerated, despite the fact that the Egyptians were always turbulent, seditious and cowardly. They were a people who had torn apart a Roman citizen because he killed a cat[13] – a people who were despised in all ages despite what admirers of the pyramids may have said about them.*

---

* This claim needs to be proved. One must accept that, since the time when history began to replace fables, the Egyptians were seen as a people who were as lazy as they were superstitious. Cambyses took control of Egypt in one single battle; Alexander imposed laws on them without meeting any opposition and without having to lay siege to a single town; the Ptolemies took control without meeting any resistance; Caesar and Augustus subdued Egypt just as easily. Omar conquered Egypt in a single campaign. The Mamelukes, a people from Colchis and the environs of Mount Caucasus, became their masters after Omar. They were the ones, rather than the Egyptians, who defeated the army of St Louis and took the king prisoner. Finally, when the Mamelukes became Egyptians – that is to say, soft, lazy, inattentive and fickle like the native inhabitants of that place – within three months they were subject to the rule of Selim I, who hanged their Sultan and left their province annexed to the Turkish empire, until other barbarians seized it some time later.

Herodotus reports that, during the time of the fables, an Egyptian named Sesostris emerged from the country with an explicit plan to conquer the universe. It is obvious that such a plan would be appropriate only for Picrochole or Don Quixote. Apart from the fact that Sesostris is not an Egyptian name, this event and all the others that preceded it are about as credible as *The Thousand and One Nights*. There is nothing more characteristic of conquered peoples than to invent fables about their ancient glory, just as destitute families in some countries pretend that they are descended from ancient sovereigns. The priests of Egypt told Herodotus stories that this king called Sesostris embarked on a campaign to subdue the Colchians; it is as if one were to say that the King of France set out from the Loire Valley to conquer Norway!

Even if these stories were repeated in thousands of volumes, they would still not be any more probable; it is much more likely that the strong and fierce inhabitants of the Caucasus, the Colchians and the other Scythians, who often succeeded in ravaging Asia, penetrated as far as Egypt. And if the priests of Colchis subsequently reported that they practised the custom of circumcision, that is no proof that the Egyptians had conquered them. Diodorus of Sicily reports that all the kings who were conquered by Sesostris came annually from the furthest regions of their kingdoms to offer tributes to him, and that Sesostris used them as horses for his carriage and that he harnessed them to his chariot when he went to the temple. The stories of *Gargantua* are faithfully copied all the time. These kings were surely good enough to travel all that distance to serve as horses in that way!

As regards the pyramids and other antiquities, they prove nothing more than the pride and poor taste of Egyptian princes, as well as the slavery of an ignorant people who used the strength of their arms – which was all they had – to satisfy the gross ostentation of their masters. The government of this people, during the very same period about which they boast so much, seems to have been absurd and tyrannical. We are told that all the lands belonged to their monarchs. These were surely the slaves who conquered the whole world!

The profound knowledge of the Egyptian priests continues to be one of the biggest jokes of ancient history (or what was really a fable). People who pretended that the Sun arose twice in the west and that it set twice in the east in the course of restarting its cycle of 11,000 years were indeed better informed than the author of the *Almanac de Liège*. The religion of these priests, who governed the State, was not even comparable to that of the most savage people of America. It is well known that they adore crocodiles, monkeys, cats and onions; and there is perhaps in the whole world today only the cult of the Dalai Lama that is as absurd.

Their art was hardly better than their religion. There is not a single ancient Egyptian statue that is worth looking at, and every item of artistic value that they possessed was made by artists from Greece in Alexandria under the Ptolemies and Caesars. They needed a Greek even to teach them geometry.

The illustrious Bossuet was enthusiastic about Egyptian talent, in his *Discours sur l'histoire universelle*, which was addressed to the son of Louis XIV. He may have impressed a young prince, but he failed to convince the learned. It was a very eloquent disquisition; but an historian should be more of a philosopher than an orator. Besides, such an interpretation of the

Was there ever anyone who was more likely to have provoked the opposition of the priests and government of Egypt
than St Gregory Thaumaturgus,[14] who was a disciple of
Origen? Gregory had seen a vision at night of an old man sent
from God, accompanied by a woman bathed in light; the
woman was the Virgin Mary and the old man was St John the
Evangelist. St John dictated a summary statement of Christianity
that St Gregory set out to preach. As he went through Neocaesarea he passed close to a temple where people consulted
oracles and in which the rain forced him to spend the night. He
made the sign of the cross several times in the temple. The next
morning the high priest of the temple was surprised to discover
that the demons that previously responded to his requests were
no longer willing to utter oracles. He summoned them, but the
demons arrived only to announce that they would not return
again. They informed him that they could no longer live in that
temple because Gregory had spent a night there and had made
the sign of the cross. The high priest seized hold of Gregory,
who replied to him: 'I am able to banish demons from any
place I wish and I can introduce them wherever I wish.' 'Then
make them return to my temple,' said the high priest. Gregory
tore a small piece of paper from the volume that he held in his
hand and he wrote the following words on it: 'I command you
to return to this temple.' This instruction was placed on the
altar. The demons obeyed and began to issue their oracles as
usual on the very same day, but, after that, as is well known,
they ceased to utter oracles there.

It was St Gregory of Nyssa who reported these events in the
Life of Gregory Thaumaturgus. The priests who consulted idols

Egyptians could not be anything more than a guess on his part, for in what
other way could we describe what is said about antiquity? [*Ed.* Cambyses II
(6th century BC) was a king of Persia who successfully invaded Egypt. Omar
was the leader of the Muslim invasion of Egypt in 640. Herodotus, *Histories*
(II, 102–10) discussed the campaign of Sesostris. Picrochole was a fictional
character created by Rabelais in *Gargantua* (1534). The *Almanac de Liège*
was widely used in the eighteenth century. Jacques-Bénigne Bossuet (1627–
1704), a Catholic bishop and theologian, was famous for his oratory. He was
also tutor to the Dauphin, to whom he dedicated his *Discours sur l'histoire
universelle* {Discourse on Universal History} (Paris, 1681).]

would certainly have had a reason to be angry with Gregory and, in their ignorance, to report him to the magistrate. Nonetheless, the great enemy of these priests experienced no persecution.

It is reported in the history of St Cyprian that he was the first bishop of Carthage who was condemned to death. The martyrdom of St Cyprian occurred in the year 258; therefore, during a very long period, no bishop of Carthage was killed because of his religion. There is no historical information about what Cyprian was accused of, who his enemies were or what provoked the proconsul for Africa against him. St Cyprian wrote to Cornelius, bishop of Rome: 'There have been public disturbances recently in Carthage and on two occasions there were calls to have me thrown to the lions.' It is very likely that the fits of anger of the ferocious Carthaginians were eventually the cause of St Cyprian's death. And it certainly was not the emperor Gallus who condemned him from afar because of his religion, because he allowed Cornelius – who lived close by – to live in peace.

There are so many hidden causes involved in observable causes, and so many unknown factors that may cause someone to be persecuted, that it is impossible after many centuries to disentangle the hidden source of the woes of the most prominent human beings, let alone the hidden explanation of why certain individuals were executed, when that is something that could have been known only by their closest associates.

Notice that St Gregory Thaumaturgus and St Dionysius, the bishop of Alexandria, who were not executed, both lived in the time of St Cyprian. Why were they allowed to live in peace, since they were at least as well known as the bishop of Carthage? And why was St Cyprian delivered up to be tortured? Does it not seem likely that he fell victim to some personal and powerful enemies, that he was the victim of a calumny that was camouflaged as if it constituted a danger to public security, which is often linked with religion, and that the other two bishops were lucky enough to have escaped the wickedness of mankind?

It is hardly possible that the accusation of being a Christian alone was a sufficient reason for St Ignatius to perish during the reign of the just and compassionate Trajan, because other Christians were allowed to accompany and console him while he was being transported to Rome.* There were often rebellions

---

* I am not casting doubt on the death of St Ignatius, but if sensible readers look at the report of his martyrdom, would they not have a number of doubts about it? The anonymous author of this report says that 'Trajan believed that there would be something lacking in his glory if he failed to subject the Christian God to his rule.' What a strange idea! Was Trajan someone who wished to conquer gods? When Ignatius appeared before the Emperor, this prince said to him: 'Who are you, impure spirit?' It is scarcely likely that the Emperor spoke to a prisoner and that he himself condemned him. That was not the way sovereigns behaved. If Trajan made Ignatius appear before him, he did not ask him 'Who are you?' since he was already well aware of who he was. Could the phrase 'impure spirit' have been used by Trajan? Is it not obvious that it is a phrase used by exorcists, which some Christian attributed to an emperor? Good God! Is that the language of Trajan?

Could one imagine Ignatius replying to him that his name was Theophorus, because he carried Jesus in his heart, and that Trajan had discussed Jesus Christ with him? Trajan was supposed to have said at the end of the discussion: 'We command that Ignatius – who is proud of carrying the crucified within himself – be put in chains, etc.' A sophistical enemy of the Christians could have called Jesus Christ 'the crucified', but it is hardly likely that such a phrase was used to pronounce a sentence. Death on a cross was so commonly used by the Romans that it would have been impossible to describe the object of the Christians' cult as 'the crucified' in the legal language of the Romans. That was not the way the emperors expressed their judgements and their laws.

St Ignatius was then said to have written a long letter to the Christians in Rome. 'I write to you,' he wrote, 'in my current condition, completely bound in chains.' Certainly, if he was allowed to write to the Christians in Rome, those Christians were therefore not exceptionally few or obscure. Trajan therefore had no intention of making their God subject to his rule; or if those Christians were already subject to persecution, Ignatius was very imprudent to write to them because that amounted to exposing them or betraying them and becoming their traitor.

It seems that those who recorded these events ought to have had greater trust in appearances and the conventions of propriety. The martyrdom of St Polycarp raises even more doubts. It is reported that a voice cried out from the highest heaven: 'Be brave, Polycarp' – and [it is reported] that the Christians heard it, but that others failed to hear it. It is said that St Polycarp was bound to the stake, and when the pyre was ablaze, the flames avoided him and formed an arch above his head, that a dove flew out from the flames, and that the saint – whom the flames avoided – gave off an aromatic odour

in Antioch, a notoriously turbulent city, where Ignatius was a clandestine bishop of the Christians. Perhaps innocent Christians were maliciously blamed for these uprisings; they may have attracted the attention of the government and its response was possibly a mistake, as often happens.

St Simeon, for example, was accused before Shapur[15] of spying for the Romans. The story of his martyrdom reports that the emperor Shapur asked him to adore the Sun. But it is well known that the Persians did not worship the Sun; they regarded it as a symbol of the source of all goodness, Ahura Mazda, of the divine creator that they acknowledged.

No matter how tolerant one may be, one cannot avoid feeling indignant at those ranters who accuse Diocletian of having persecuted Christians from the day he ascended the throne. Let us hear what Eusebius of Caesarea says about them, since his testimony cannot be doubted. The favourite and eulogist of Constantine,[16] who was a fierce enemy of all previous emperors, should be believed when he justifies their actions. Here is what he wrote:* 'The emperors showed signs of benevolence towards Christians for a long time. They entrusted provinces to them. Many Christians lived in the palace and they even married Christian women. Diocletian chose Prisca as his wife, whose daughter was the wife of Maximianus Galerius, and so on.'

One should learn from this decisive testimony never to resort to calumny, and one should decide if the persecution that Galerius initiated – after nineteen years of a compassionate and beneficent reign – must have been caused by some intrigue about which we know nothing.

One should also see how much the fable about the Theban Legion, the members of which were said to have been completely massacred because of their religion, is an absurd fable.[17] It is ridiculous to suggest that they arranged to have this legion

---

which enveloped all those who stood nearby, but that he whom the flames refused to approach was unable to survive the sharp edge of a sword. One must acknowledge that we should forgive those who find more piety than truth in such stories. [*Ed.* Polycarp, a disciple of John the Apostle and a bishop of Smyrna, was burnt at the stake between 155 and 157.]

* *Ecclesiastical History*, Book VIII.

return from Asia through the Great St Bernard Pass. It is impossible that it would have been recalled from Asia to restore peace during an insurrection among the Gauls, a full year after the same uprising had been suppressed. It is equally impossible that 6,000 infantry and 700 cavalry were slaughtered in a narrow pass where 200 men could halt the advance of an entire army. The story about this alleged butchery begins: 'When the earth groaned under Diocletian's tyranny, Heaven was filled with martyrs.' This event, as reported, was supposed to have occurred in 286, when Diocletian was most favourably disposed to Christians and the Roman Empire was most at peace. Finally, one fact that ought to save us from all these disputes is that there never was a Theban legion. The Romans were too proud and too sensible to have formed a legion that was composed of Egyptians who were useful to Rome only as slaves, *Verna Canopi*.[18] It was as unlikely as if they had formed a Jewish legion! We have the names of thirty-two legions, which constituted the principal forces of the Roman Empire, and there is certainly no mention of a Theban legion among them. So let us file this story among the acrostic verses of the Sibyls who predicted the miracles of Jesus Christ, and with so many other imagined stories that a misguided zeal invents in order to exploit the credulity of people.

TEN

The Danger of False Legends and Persecution

Lies have dominated people for a long time. It is now time to get to know the few truths that can be extracted from the clouds of fables that have obscured Roman history since Tacitus and Suetonius and have almost always enveloped the annals of other ancient nations.

For example, how could someone believe that the Romans – a serious and solemn people from whom we inherited our laws – condemned to prostitution Christian virgins who were daughters of respectable families? That would imply that one knows very little about the austere dignity of those who founded our laws and who punished so severely any failings among the Vestals. The *Sincere Acts* of Ruinart report those depraved events.[1] But should we trust the *Acts* of Ruinart as much as the Acts of the Apostles? Those *Sincere Acts*, which were based on Bolland, say that there were seven Christian virgins in the city of Ancyra,[2] each of whom was about seventy years old, and that they were sentenced by the governor Theodectus to surrender to the lust of young men of that city. But when these virgins were spared (as one would expect), he forced them to attend the mysteries of Diana while they were completely naked, although no one ever participated in those mysteries without a veil. St Theodotus, who in fact was an innkeeper but was no less zealous because of that, prayed ardently and asked God to allow these holy women to die, because he feared that they might succumb to temptation. God granted his prayer. The governor then had them thrown into a lake with stones around their necks. They appeared immediately afterwards to Theodotus and asked him not to allow their bodies to be eaten by the fish. Those were their very own words.

During the night, the holy innkeeper and his companions went to the lakeside, which was guarded by soldiers. A heavenly torch moved before them constantly and when they reached the place that was guarded by soldiers a heavenly horseman, fully armed, pursued the soldiers with his lance. St Theodotus retrieved the bodies of the virgins from the lake. He was later brought before the governor, but the heavenly horseman did not prevent him from being decapitated. Let us never cease to repeat that we do indeed venerate genuine martyrs, but it is difficult to believe this story from Bolland and Ruinart.

Is it necessary to repeat here the story of the young St Romanus?[3] He was thrown into a fire, says Eusebius, and some Jews who were present insulted Jesus Christ because he allowed those who confessed their faith in him to be burned, whereas God had rescued Sidrach, Misach and Abdenago from a fiery furnace.[4] The Jews had hardly spoken when St Romanus emerged triumphant from the flames. The Emperor ordered that he be pardoned and he told the judge that he did not wish to get involved in any way with God (strange words for Diocletian!). The judge, however, despite the Emperor's clemency, ordered that St Romanus have his tongue cut out and, although he had executioners available, he had that operation done by a medical doctor. The young Romanus, who had suffered from a stutter from birth, spoke fluently once his tongue had been cut out. The doctor felt as if he had been reprimanded and, to show that he had performed the operation in accordance with medical practice, he grabbed a passer-by and cut out his tongue in the same way as he had operated on St Romanus, as a result of which the passer-by dropped dead immediately. 'For,' the learned author added, 'anatomy teaches us that one cannot survive without a tongue.'[5] If Eusebius had written that kind of nonsense, and if others had not added this story to his writings, how could we trust his *History*?

We have been told about the martyrdom of St Felicity[6] and her seven children, who were said to have been sent to their

deaths by the wise and dutiful Antoninus, although the author
of the report is unknown.

It is very likely that some author who was more zealous
than truthful wished to emulate the story about the Maccabees.[7] This is how the report begins: 'St Felicity was a Roman
woman, who lived during the reign of Antoninus.' It is clear
from this choice of words that the author was not a contemporary of St Felicity. He says that the Praetor pronounced his
judgement at his court on the Campus Martius, although the
prefect of Rome held court at the Capitol, and not at the Campus Martius, which had been used originally for assemblies
known as *comitia* and was subsequently used for military
parades, horse races and military games. That alone shows
that this story of martyrdom is a fable.

He also says that, once the judgement was delivered, the
Emperor assigned responsibility to different judges to carry out
the sentence, which is completely contrary to all the practices
that applied in that period and at all other times.

There was also a certain St Hippolytus,[8] who is supposed to
have been drawn by horses, as was Hippolytus the son of Theseus. The ancient Romans never used this kind of execution,
and the mere fact that their names were similar inspired someone to invent the story.

We should also notice that in the reports of martyrdom that
were composed exclusively by the Christians themselves there
is almost always a group of Christians who enter freely into
the prison of the condemned person, accompany him or her to
their execution, collect their blood, bury their body and perform miracles with their relics. If they had persecuted martyrs
only because of their religion, would they not also have taken
the lives of these professed Christians who assisted their condemned colleagues and who were accused of performing magic
with the remains of the martyrs' bodies? Would they not have
treated them as we treated the Waldensians, Albigensians,
Hussites and other Protestant sects? We slaughtered them and
burned them en masse without distinction of age or gender.
Among the reliable reports of ancient persecutions, was there
ever a single example that was comparable to that of St

Bartholomew or the massacres in Ireland? Was there ever anything like the annual festival that they still celebrate in Toulouse, during which the whole population thanks God in a procession and congratulates its ancestors for having massacred 4,000 of their fellow citizens two centuries ago?

I say this in horror, but also in truth: it is we ourselves, we Christians, who have been persecutors, executioners and assassins! And of whom? Our fellow Christians. It is we who have destroyed a hundred towns, with the crucifix or the Bible[9] in our hands, and who have never ceased to spill blood and light faggots at the stake, from the reign of Constantine to the terrors of the cannibals who lived in the Cévennes.[10] These were appalling events that, thank God, have not continued in our own day.

Sometimes we still send to the gallows unfortunate people from Poitou, Vivarais, Valence or Montauban. Since 1745 we have hanged eight of the people who are called preachers or evangelists, whose only crime was to have prayed to God for the king in their local dialect and to have given a drop of wine and a small piece of leavened bread to a few ignorant peasants.[11] They know nothing about this in Paris, where pleasure is the only important thing and where they ignore anything that occurs in the provinces or abroad. These trials are completed in an hour, more quickly than the time it takes to decide the fate of a deserter from the army. If the king were informed about them, he would grant them a pardon.

Catholic priests are not treated that way in any Protestant country. There are more than a hundred Catholic priests in England and Ireland; their identities are known, and yet they were allowed to live peacefully during the recent war.[12]

Will we always be the last ones to adopt the sane policies of other nations? They have corrected their mistakes; when will we do likewise? It took sixty years for us to accept what Newton had demonstrated;[13] we are just beginning to have the courage to save our children's lives by inoculation;[14] we have only recently begun to implement the true principles of agriculture in France; when will we begin to practise the true principles of humanity? And how can we reproach pagans for

having turned Christians into martyrs as long as we are guilty
of the same cruelty in similar circumstances?

Let us assume that the Romans caused the death of a large
number of Christians because of their religious faith. If that is
true, the Romans were very blameworthy. Do we wish to commit the same injustice? And while we blame them for having
persecuted Christians, would we wish to do the same thing?

If there is anyone so lacking in good faith or so fanatical as
to ask me, at this point: why do you come along to expose our
mistakes and our faults? Why do you destroy our false miracles and false legends? They nourish the piety of many people
and some errors are unavoidable. You should not remove an
old ulcer from the body if its removal could destroy the body.
This is how I would reply to someone like that.

All the false miracles by which you undermine our faith in
genuine miracles, all those absurd legends that you add to the
truths of the Gospel, extinguish religious belief in human
hearts. There are too many people who wish to educate themselves but lack the time to do so adequately and who then
conclude: the ministers of my religion have deceived me and
therefore there is no religion. It is better to trust in what we
learn from nature than in what we learn from religion; I prefer
to rely on natural law than on human fictions. Other people
are unfortunate enough to go much further. They realize that
deception has restrained them and they do not accept even the
restraint of what is true; consequently, they lean towards atheism. They become depraved because others were cruel and
deceitful.

These are certainly the consequences of all that pious fraud
and superstition. People usually make only a limited use of
their reason. It is very poor logic to argue as follows: Varazze,
author of the *Golden Legends*,[15] and the Jesuit Ribadeneira,
who compiled the *Flower of the Saints*,[16] have written only
silly things; therefore there is no God. Catholics have executed
a certain number of Huguenots and Huguenots, in turn, have
assassinated a certain number of Catholics, and therefore there
is no God. People have exploited confession, communion and
all the sacraments to commit the most appalling crimes;

therefore there is no God. I would conclude, on the contrary: therefore, there is a God who, after this short life, during which we have misunderstood Him so much and committed so many crimes in His name, will deign to console us for so many horrible misfortunes. For if one considered the wars of religion and the forty papal schisms, nearly all of which were bloody; the deceptions, nearly all of which have been fatal; the irreconcilable hatreds that were inflamed by differences of opinion; and if one considered all the evils that result from false zeal, one would conclude that human beings have been suffering hell on Earth for a very long time.

ELEVEN

The Abuse of Intolerance

But will every citizen then be allowed to believe their own unaided reason and to think whatever their own reason tells them, whether it is enlightened or misguided? Yes, that should be allowed* on condition that it does not disturb public order, because people are not obliged to believe or not believe certain things, but are obliged to respect the customs of their own country. And if Catholics were to say that it is a crime not to believe in the dominant religion, that would simply amount to accusing the first Christians, who were their own ancestors, and justifying those whom they accuse of having delivered them to be executed.

You may answer that there is a big difference between the two cases, and that all other religions are human inventions, while the Catholic, apostolic and Roman Church alone is the work of God. But, in good faith, should our religion reign by hatred, terror, banishments, torture and murders, and by using murder to give thanks to God just because it is divine? Insofar as the Christian religion is divine, human beings should not get involved in enforcing it. If God is truly the author of our religion, God will sustain it without your help. You know that intolerance produces only hypocrites or rebels – what a fatal choice! Finally, do you wish to use executioners to support the

* See Locke's excellent *Letter* about toleration. [*Ed.* John Locke (1632–1704) wrote the *Epistola de Tolerantia* to a Dutch friend, Philip von Limborch in 1685, and it was published anonymously in the United Provinces in 1689; it was translated into English by William Popple and published in London as *A Letter concerning Toleration* (1689), and subsequently into French (1710).]

religion of a God whose death was caused by execution and who preached only gentleness and patience?

I implore you to consider the appalling consequences of a law of intolerance. If a society legislated for a specific level of toleration, and if it allowed citizens who fail to profess a religion that falls within those legal limits to be stripped of their goods, to be thrown into dungeons or to be killed, what exception would exempt the leaders of the State from such punishments? Religion is equally binding on a monarch and a beggar. Besides, more than fifty learned men or monks have taught the monstrous doctrine that it is permissible to depose and kill sovereigns who do not believe what the dominant church believes, and the *parlements* of the kingdom have never ceased to proscribe those abominable decisions of abominable theologians.*

---

* The Jesuit Busenbaum, on whose work another Jesuit called Lacroix provided a commentary, says that 'it is permissible to kill a prince who is excommunicated by the Pope, in any country in which such a prince is found, and that whoever carries out this commission performs an act of charity.' That proposition, which was formulated in the depths of Hell, was the main reason why the whole of France was opposed to the Jesuits. They were reproached more than ever before for this dogma, which they had so often defended and so often disavowed. They thought they could justify themselves by finding approximately the same doctrine in St Thomas and a number of Dominicans. (Consult, if you can, the *Letter of a Worldly Man to a Theologian, concerning St Thomas*; it's a pamphlet by a Jesuit, from 1762.) In fact, St Thomas Aquinas, the angelic doctor and the interpreter of God's will (such are his titles), proposes that an apostate prince loses his right to govern and that he should no longer be obeyed; that the Church may punish him with death (Bk II, part ii, question 12); that the emperor Julian was tolerated only because he was more powerful than everyone else (ibid.); that, as a matter of law, every heretic should be killed (ibid., questions 11, 12); that those who liberate the people from a tyrannical prince are very praiseworthy; etc., etc. The 'angelic doctor' is very much respected. But if he had come to France to teach such doctrines during the age of Jacques Clément or his colleague the Feuillant Ravaillac how would the 'angelic doctor' have been treated?

One must acknowledge that Jean Gerson, the Chancellor of the University of Paris, went even further than St Thomas and that the Cordelier Jean Petit went infinitely further still. Many Cordeliers defended the appalling theses of Jean Petit. One must admit that this diabolical doctrine of regicide originates exclusively in the foolish idea that all monks had accepted for a long time, namely that the Pope is God on Earth, who may dispose arbitrarily of the thrones and

Henry the Great had only just died when the Paris *parlement* issued its ruling that established the independence of the Crown as a basic law. Cardinal Duperron, who owed his cardinal's hat to Henry the Great, opposed this ruling in the Estates in 1614 and caused its suppression.[1] All the journals of the period report the words that Duperron used in his speeches: 'If a prince were to become an Arian,' he said, 'one would be obliged to depose him.'

Certainly not, Mr Cardinal. Let us consider your chimerical assumption that one of our kings had read the history of the Church councils and the Fathers of the Church and that he was struck by these words: 'My Father is greater than me.'[2] If he understood them too literally and was weighing up the Councils of Nicaea and Constantinople, and if he decided in favour of Eusebius of Nicomedia,[3] I would not obey my king any less; I would not think I was less bound by the oath that I had made to him. And if you dared to rebel against him and if I were one of your judges, I would find you guilty of treason.

I summarize the disputation that Duperron continued at great length, for this is not the right place to examine in detail those revolting fantasies. I shall say no more than this, in which

---

lives of kings. That belief is even worse than when the Tartars believe that the Dalai Lama is immortal. He distributes among them samples from his commode; they dry them as relics, enshrine them and kiss them devoutly. For my part I would much prefer, for the sake of peace, to carry such relics around my neck than to believe that the Pope has the slightest jurisdiction over the temporal power of kings or even over my civil rights, in whatever situation I may find myself. [*Ed.* Hermann Busenbaum (1600–1668) was the Jesuit author of *Medulla theologiae moralis facili ac perspicua methodo resolvens casus conscientiae* {A Summary of Moral Philosophy with an Easy and Perspicuous Method for Resolving Questions of Conscience} (Brussels, 1645); Claude Lacroix (1652–1714), another Jesuit, published a commentary on the *Medulla* as *Theologia moralis* {Moral Theology} (Cologne, 1719), in which the section on regicide was expanded. St Thomas discusses the issues raised by Voltaire in the *Summa theologiae*, IIa IIae, q. 11, art. 3 (heretics may be put to death), and q. 12, art. 2 (subjects may refuse allegiance to apostate kings). Jean Charlier de Gerson (1363–1429) was Chancellor of the University of Paris and a famous defender of conciliarism when three different people claimed simultaneously to be Pope. He argued against the writings of Jean Petit (*c.* 1360–1411), which attempted to justify the murder of the king's brother, the Duke of Orléans.]

I agree with all other citizens: we owe obedience to Henry IV, not because he was consecrated king at the cathedral of Chartres, but because the incontrovertible law of birth granted the crown to this prince, who deserved it because of his courage and his goodness.

I wish to say, if I may, that all citizens should inherit their father's possessions by the same law, and that we do not see how a citizen could deserve to be deprived of their inheritance and to be dragged off to the gallows because they share the opinion of Ratramnus against Paschasius Radbertus or that of Berengarius against Scotus.[4]

It is well known that all our dogmas were not always explained clearly and accepted universally in our Church. Since Jesus Christ did not reveal how the Holy Spirit proceeded, the Latin Church believed for a long time (as did the Greek Church) that the Holy Spirit proceeded only from God the Father; later it added to the official creed that he also proceeded from God the Son.[5] On the day after the Church had made that decision, I wonder if a citizen who accepted the creed of the previous day deserved the death penalty? Would it be any less cruel and unjust to punish someone today who believes what we used to believe in former times? Was it blameworthy, during the papacy of Honorius I,[6] to believe that Jesus Christ did not have two wills?

It is only a short time since the Church began to teach the doctrine of the Immaculate Conception.[7] The Dominicans still do not believe it. At what point will the Dominicans deserve to be punished in this life and in the next?

If there is anyone from whom we ought to learn and by whom we ought to be guided in our interminable disputes, it is certainly the apostles and the evangelists. The disagreement between St Peter and St Paul was serious enough to have provoked a violent schism. Paul says explicitly in his Epistle to the Galatians that he confronted Peter face to face because Peter was reprehensible for having resorted to deception with Barnabas; he dined with Gentiles before James had arrived and then withdrew secretly and deserted the Gentiles for fear of offending those who were circumcised. 'But when I saw,' he added, 'that they walked not uprightly unto the truth of the gospel, I said to Cephas[8] before them all: If thou, being a Jew, livest after the manner of the Gentiles, and not as the Jews do, how dost thou compel the Gentiles to live as do the Jews?'[9]

That was an issue that provoked a violent dispute. The question was whether or not new Christians should observe Jewish rituals. St Paul went to the temple of Jerusalem to offer sacrifice during that very period.[10] We know that the first fifteen bishops of Jerusalem were circumcised Jews who observed the Sabbath and abstained from forbidden foods. If a Spanish or Portuguese bishop were to have himself circumcised and to observe the Sabbath today, he would be burned at the stake as an act of penance. Nonetheless, this fundamental issue did not disturb the peace of the early Church, either among the apostles or among the early Christians.

If the evangelists had been like modern authors, they would have had quite a large number of things about which to dispute with each other. St Matthew counts twenty-eight generations from David to Jesus; St Luke counts forty-one generations, and they are completely different.[11] Nonetheless, the disciples did not dispute about these apparent contradictions, which were reconciled by a number of Church Fathers. They did not breach the demands of charity and they preserved the peace. Where else would we get a better lesson about tolerating each other when we disagree and about being humble about things that we do not understand?

St Paul, in the epistle he wrote to certain Jews in Rome who had converted to Christianity, devotes the whole conclusion of the third chapter to saying that faith alone glorifies us and that works never justify anyone.[12] St James, on the contrary, in his epistle to twelve tribes who were scattered throughout the world (Chapter 2) never stops saying that one cannot be saved without works.[13] That is what divides two great Christian communions in our day, although it did not cause any division among the apostles.

If it were saintly to persecute those with whom we disagree, it would follow that whoever killed the most heretics would be the greatest saint in Paradise. If someone were content merely to despoil his fellow citizens and throw them into dungeons, how would such a person compare in Heaven when placed next to a zealot who had massacred hundreds of people on St Bartholomew's Day? Here is the proof of that.

Each successor of St Peter together with his consistory of cardinals is infallible. They approved, celebrated and consecrated the St Bartholomew Massacre. Therefore, that was a holy action. If we compare two murderers who are equally pious, therefore, the one who disembowels twenty-four pregnant Huguenot women should be glorified twice as much as one who disembowels only twelve. By the same reasoning, the fanatics of the Cévennes should believe that they would be glorified in proportion to the number of priests, religious and Christian women that they slaughtered. Those are strange reasons indeed for claiming eternal glory.

TWELVE

Was Intolerance Part of Divine Law in Judaism and was it always Practised?

I think that the commandments that were given by God Himself are called 'divine law'. God commanded the Jews to eat a lamb cooked with lettuce, and that guests should eat while standing and holding a staff in their hands in memory of the Passover.[1] He commanded that the high priest be consecrated by putting blood on his right ear, his right hand and right foot.[2] These appear to us to be extraordinary customs, but not so to antiquity. God ordered the Jewish people to transfer all their iniquities to the goat Hazazel;[3] he forbade them to eat fish without scales, pork, hares, hedgehogs, owls, vultures, kites, etc.*

God established festivals and ceremonies. All these things, which appear arbitrary to other nations where they are subject to positive laws and custom, became divine law for the Jews once they were commanded by God, just as everything that Jesus Christ, the son of Mary and Son of God, commanded us has become divine law for us.

We shall not inquire here why God substituted a new law for the law that He had given to Moses, nor why He gave more commandments to Moses than to the patriarch Abraham, and more to Abraham than to Noah.† He seems to have decided to

---

* Deuteronomy 14. [*Ed.* The corresponding text in Leviticus 11:13–14 lists the same birds of prey that were forbidden, but without any mention of an *ixion*, which is translated above as 'kite'. The Hebrew text may have been corrupted, so that the precise meaning of the term remains uncertain.]

† Since I planned to provide some useful notes in this work, I shall point out here that God was said to have made a covenant with Noah and all the animals. Nonetheless, He allowed Noah to eat 'anything that was alive and moved'. The only exception was blood, which people were not allowed to use

as food. God added that He 'would take revenge against any animals that spilled human blood'.

These and many other passages imply that the whole of antiquity and all sensible people believed, up to now, that animals had some kind of knowledge. God did not make a covenant with plants and stones, which had no sensations; but He did make a covenant with animals, which He thought were endowed with sensations that were often more acute than ours and with the ideas that were attached to those sensations. That is why He did not approve the kind of barbarity involved in being nourished by blood, because blood is effectively the source of life and therefore of sensation. That is why Scripture very reasonably says, in a hundred places, that the soul – in other words, what is called the sentient soul – is in the blood. That was the very natural view that all peoples held in the past.

The compassion that we should have for animals is based on this opinion. Among the seven commandments of the Noahides, which were adopted by the Jews, there is one that prohibits eating part of a living animal. This commandment shows that human beings were cruel enough to mutilate animals in order to eat parts of them that they had cut off, and that they allowed them to continue living so that they could subsequently eat other parts of their bodies. This custom was prevalent among a number of barbaric peoples, as is evident in the sacrifices to Bacchus Omadius (the one who eats raw flesh) on the island of Chios. Thus when God allowed us to use animals as food, He recommended that we be humane towards them. One must agree that it is barbaric to cause them suffering. It is certainly true that custom is the only thing that could reduce our natural abhorrence of slaughtering any animal that we have reared ourselves. There were always people who were very scrupulous about that. This scruple survives today in the Indian peninsula; all the disciples of Pythagoras, in Italy and Greece, abstain completely from eating meat. Porphyry, in his book *Abstinence*, reproaches one of his disciples for leaving their sect simply to satisfy his barbarous appetite.

It seems to me that one would have to abandon the natural light of reason to dare believe that animals are mere machines. There is a manifest contradiction in holding that God gave animals all the organs for sensations and that He failed to give them sensations.

I also think that it would be necessary not to have ever observed animals in order not to distinguish their different expressions of need, suffering, joy, fear, love, anger and all their feelings. It would be very strange if they were so successful at expressing something that they do not sense.

This comment would provide much food for thought for minds that reflect on the power and goodness of the Creator, who deigned to bestow life, sensation, ideas and memory on beings that He Himself had designed by using His omnipotent creativity. We do not know how these organs were formed nor how they developed; we do not know the laws that bind sensations, ideas, memory and the will to these living things. And in this profound and eternal ignorance, which is inherent in our nature, we dispute endlessly and adapt the law to different historical periods and to the expansion of the human race. This is legislation on a paternal scale. But these deep issues are too profound for our feeble understanding. Let us therefore stay within the limits of our subject matter and let us consider first if the Jews were intolerant.

It is true that there are very severe laws about religious observance and even more severe penalties in Exodus, Numbers, Leviticus and Deuteronomy. Many commentators have found it difficult to reconcile what Moses records with passages in Jeremiah and Amos, and with the well-known speech of St Stephen that is reported in the Acts of the Apostles. Amos says that the Jews adored Moloch, Rempham and Chiun during the whole time they were in the desert.* Jeremiah says explicitly that God did not request any sacrifice from their forefathers when they were leaving Egypt.† St Stephen, in his speech to the Jews, says the following:‡ 'They adored the host of Heaven, they did not offer any sacrifice or slain victims in the desert during a period of forty years; they carried the tabernacle of the god Moloch, and the star of their god Rempham.'

---

persecute each other, like bulls that batter each other with their horns without knowing why or how they have such horns in the first place.

[*Ed.* The first quotation is from Genesis 9:3. There was a legend that the inhabitants of the island of Chios (a Greek island off the coast of modern Turkey) offered human sacrifices to Bacchus (Dionysus), to whom they gave the surname Omadius because he accepted sacrifices that included human mutilation. Pythagoras (*c.* 570–*c.* 490 BC) was one of the most famous Presocratic Greek philosophers. He emigrated to Croton in southern Italy and founded a school there; he was reported as not eating meat. Porphyry (*c.* 234–*c.* 305), born in Tyre, was a Neoplatonist and author of a life of Plotinus. He wrote *De abstinentia ab animalibus necandi* {*On Abstinence from Killing Animals*} (trans. G. Clark: London: Duckworth, 2000), in which he reproached Firmus for abandoning vegetarianism. The final sections of this note reflect a misunderstanding of the Cartesian theory of animal behaviour; in fact, Descartes did not deny sentience or memory in animals, but claimed merely that the explanation of these sensations in animals or human beings did not require postulating a spiritual soul.]

* Amos 5:26.
† Jeremiah 7:22.
‡ Acts 7:42–3.

From the fact that they worshipped so many foreign gods, other critics conclude that Moses tolerated these gods, and to support that interpretation they quote the following words from Deuteronomy:* 'When you are in the land of Chanaan, you will not do as we do now, when everyone does whatever they themselves believe is good.'†

---

* Deuteronomy 12:8.

† Several writers conclude too confidently from this passage that the chapter about the golden calf (which was the same thing as Apis, the god of the Nile) was added to the books of Moses, together with many other chapters.

Ibn Ezra was the first to think he could prove that the Pentateuch was composed during the period of the kings. Wollaston, Collins, Tindal, Shaftesbury, Bolingbroke and many others have claimed that the art of writing on polished stone, on tiles, lead or wood was the only form of writing that was available in that period. They say that, since the time of Moses, the Chaldeans and Egyptians wrote only in that way; that it was impossible to write in that era except by expressing the essence of what one wished to pass on to posterity in a very abbreviated style, in hieroglyphics rather than in detailed histories. They say that it was impossible to have written a long book in a desert, when people often moved to new locations where there was no one who could supply and fit clothes or even mend sandals, and where God had to work a forty-year miracle to conserve the clothes and shoes of His people. They say that it is unlikely that they had many people who could engrave letters when they lacked the most basic skills and could not even bake bread. And if these commentators are told that the columns of the tabernacle were made of bronze and the capitals of the columns were solid silver, they reply that these building instructions may have been given earlier when the Jews were in the desert and that they were implemented only later in more prosperous times.

These commentators cannot conceive of this impoverished people asking to adore a golden calf at the foot of the very mountain where God had spoken to Moses, in the middle of a storm with thunder and lightning and while they heard the sound of a heavenly trumpet. They are surprised that, even on the very day before Moses descended from the mountain, all the people asked the brother of Moses to get this great golden calf. How did Aaron cast it in a foundry in a single day? How did Moses then reduce it to dust? They say that it is impossible for any artist to make a golden statue in less than three months, and that it would be impossible even for the most scholarly chemist to reduce it to dust that is fine enough to be swallowed. For that reason, the transgression of Aaron and the work of Moses would be a double miracle.

Their humanity and goodwill, which misleads them, prevents them from believing that Moses had 23,000 people slaughtered to expiate this sin. They do not think that 23,000 people would have allowed themselves to be massacred by Levites, which would be at least a third miracle. Finally, they find it strange that Aaron, who was the most blameworthy of all, was rewarded for a crime for which the others were punished so horribly, and that he was made a high priest while the corpses of his bloodstained brothers were piled at the foot of the altar where he went to offer sacrifice.

They have the same concern about the 24,000 Israelites who were massacred on the orders of Moses in order to expiate the sin of just one man who had been found with a Madianite girl. There were so many Jewish kings, especially Solomon, who married foreign women with impunity that these critics cannot accept that a relationship with a Madianite was such a great crime. Ruth was a Moabite, although her family came originally from Bethlehem; Holy Scripture always refers to Ruth as a Moabite. Nonetheless, she went to the bed of Boaz on the advice of her mother-in-law; she received six bushels of barley from him, and then married him and became the grandmother of David. Rahab was not only a foreigner but a woman of the street; the only title that the Vulgate gives her is 'harlot'. She married Salmon, the prince of Judah, and this Salmon was also the one from whom David descended. Rahab is even taken as a symbol of the Christian Church; that was the interpretation of many Fathers of the Church, especially of Origen in his seventh homily on the Book of Joshua.

Bethsabee, the wife of Uriah, by whom David had Solomon, was a Hittite. If you go back further in this ancestry, the patriarch Judah married a Canaanite woman, and his children married Tamar of the tribe of Aram. This woman, with whom Judah unintentionally committed incest, was not an Israelite.

Thus our Saviour Jesus Christ deigned to be incarnated among the Jews in a family that had five foreign ancestors in order to show that foreign nations would share in his inheritance.

The rabbi Ibn Esra was, as I mentioned, the first one to dare claim that the Pentateuch was composed a long time after Moses. He based his conclusion on many passages. 'The Canaanite was already in that land. The mountain of Moriah was called God's mountain. The bedstead of Og, king of Bashan, may still be seen in Rabath, and he calls this whole land of Bashan the towns of Jair up to our own time. There was never seen again in Israel a prophet like Moses. These are the kings who ruled in Edom before any king ruled in Israel.' He claims that these passages, which refer to events that occurred after the time of Moses, could not be attributed to Moses. Others think that these passages were notes that were added by copyists a long time later.

Newton, whose name should be mentioned only with respect, but who was fallible because he was human, attributes the books of Moses, Joshua and Judges to much later sacred authors in his introduction to his commentaries on Daniel and St John. He bases his interpretation on Genesis 36; on four chapters of Judges, 17, 18, 19, 21; Samuel 8; Chronicles 2; the Book of Ruth 4. In fact, if they spoke about kings in Genesis 36, if they mention kings in the Book of Judges, and if they speak about David in the Book of Ruth, it seems as if all these books were composed in the time of the kings. That is also the opinion of some theologians, foremost among whom is the famous Leclerc. But there are only a few people who adopt that interpretation, whose curiosity reaches into those depths of scholarship. There is no doubt that we should not include that degree of curiosity among our duties. When the learned and the uneducated, princes and shepherds, appear after this brief life before the Lord of eternity, each one of us will then wish to be just, humane, compassionate and generous. None of us will boast that we knew precisely in what year the Pentateuch was written or that we had disentangled the original text from notes that were added by scribes. God will not ask us if we had sided with the Massorites against the Talmud, if we had ever mistaken a Kaph for a Beth, a Yod for a Waw or a Daleth for a Resh. He will certainly judge us by our actions, and not by our understanding of the Hebrew language. We will hold firmly to the Church's decision on these matters, in accordance with the reasonable duty of faithful members.

Let us conclude this note with an important passage from Leviticus, a book that was composed after the adoration of the golden calf. God commanded the Jews not to adore animals (Leviticus 17), 'the same goats with which they had committed infamous abominations'. It is not known if this strange cult originated in Egypt, which is a country of superstition and magical spells. But it is believed that the habit of our would-be sorcerers, of attending a sabbath and adoring a goat there, and of abandoning oneself to inconceivable turpitudes with a goat – the very idea of which is horrifying – came from the ancient Jews. In fact, they were the ones who taught sorcery in parts of Europe. What a people! Such a strange infamy would seem to deserve a punishment comparable to what they suffered as a result of the golden calf. Nonetheless, the [divine] lawgiver was content to provide them with a simple prohibition. I report this fact here only to inform readers about the Jewish nation. Bestiality must have been common among them (Leviticus 18:23), because it is the only nation where we know the laws had to prohibit a crime that was not suspected elsewhere by any other legislators.

One could believe that, given the stresses and penury that the Jews suffered in the deserts of Paran, Horeb and Kadesh-Barnea, the women – who were weaker than the men – died out. The Jews must certainly have missed girls, because they were always ordered, when they captured a town or village, either on the left or right bank of the Dead Sea, to kill everyone except the nubile girls.

The Arabs who still live in these deserts always stipulate, in the treaties they make with caravans, that they are to be given nubile girls. It is likely that young people, in that dreadful country, had stretched the depravity of human nature as far as copulating with goats, as is reported about some shepherds of Calabria. It remains to be seen if these matings resulted in the birth of monsters and if there is any basis for the ancient stories about satyrs, fauns, centaurs and minotaurs. History reports these events, but science has not yet enlightened us about this monstrous thing.

They base their interpretation on the fact that there is no mention of any religious activity among the people when they were in the desert – no celebration of Passover, no Pentecost, no indication that they celebrated the feast of the tabernacles and no established public prayers. Finally, they did not practise circumcision, which was the hallmark of their covenant with God.

They rely even more on the history of Joshua. This conqueror says to the Jews: 'You have a choice: choose whichever you wish, either to adore the gods that you served in the land of the Amorites or those that you recognized in Mesopotamia.'* The people replied: 'That is not the way it is. We shall serve Adonai.' Joshua replied to them: 'You have made your own choice. You must therefore remove foreign gods from your

---

[*Ed.* Abraham ibn Ezra (1089–1167) was a famous Spanish Jewish scholar. The quotation from Ibn Ezra includes six quotations from the Old Testament: Genesis 12:6, 22:2; Deuteronomy 3:11, 14, 34:10; Genesis 36:31. The period of the kings was from 1050 to 586 BC. Voltaire refers to five British deists as authors who cast doubt on literal interpretations of texts from the Old Testament. William Wollaston (1659–1724) was most famous for *The Religion of Nature Delineated* (1722). Anthony Collins (1676–1729) wrote, among other works, *A Discourse on the Grounds and Reasons of the Christian Religion* (1724); Matthew Tindal (1657–1733) was the author of *Christianity as Old as the Creation* (1730); Anthony Ashley Cooper, 3rd Earl of Shaftesbury (1671–1713) was the author of *Characteristics of Men, Manners, Opinions, Times* (1711); Henry St John, 1st Viscount Bolingbroke (1678–1751) was a contemporary and friend of Voltaire who published studies on the dating of biblical books, *Philosophical Works* (1754). The book by Isaac Newton is *Observations upon the prophecies of Daniel, and the Apocalypse of St John, in two parts* (1733). The 'famous Leclerc' was Jean Leclerc (1657–1736), one of the founders of modern critical biblical studies. The Massorites were biblical scholars who specialized in copying and passing on authentic versions of the Old Testament books. Kaph, Beth, etc., are pairs of letters of the Hebrew alphabet that are sufficiently similar that one might confuse one with another. Voltaire seems to have borrowed stories about copulating with goats from Jean Bodin's *De la démonomanie des sorciers* {On the Demon-Mania of Witches} (Paris, 1580). It is not clear why he thought the alleged practices of sorcerers were taught by Jews. The three deserts listed are mentioned frequently in the Old Testament; Paran is where the Jews wandered for forty years; Horeb or Oreb was the location of Mount Sinai, where Moses received the Ten Commandments; and Kadesh-Barnea was on the border of Palestine, close to the Promised Land.]

* Joshua 24:15ff.

midst.' Therefore, they must have had gods other than Adonai in the time of Moses.

It is completely useless in this context to refute critics who think that Moses did not write the Pentateuch. Everything about this question has already been said a long time ago. And even if some small part of the books of Moses had been written during the time of the judges or the kings, they would not be any less inspired or sacred for that reason.

It seems to me that it is enough if Holy Scripture shows that, despite the extraordinary punishment that the Jews suffered because of their cult of Apis, they retained great freedom of worship for a long time. It is even possible that the massacre of 23,000 people by Moses because of the calf that had been erected by his brother made him realize that nothing is gained by severe punishment, and that he had to turn a blind eye to the people's passion for foreign gods.

He himself seems to have broken the law that he delivered.* He forbade all images and, nonetheless, he erected a bronze serpent. There was a similar exception from the law at a later date in the temple of Solomon. This prince had sculpted a dozen oxen to support the great pool of the temple;[4] Cherubim were placed over the Ark of the Covenant; they had an eagle's head and a calf's head; and it is apparently this calf's head, which was poorly made, that was found by Roman soldiers in the temple, as a result of which people believed for a long time that the Jews adored a donkey.

The prohibition of the cult of foreign or strange gods was ineffective. Solomon was discreetly an idolater. Jeroboam, to whom God gave ten parts of the kingdom, had two golden calves erected and he reigned for twenty-two years by uniting in himself the offices of monarch and pontiff.[5] The small kingdom of Judah erected strange altars and statues during Roboam's reign.[6] The holy king Asa did not destroy the high places.[7] The high priest Urias erected an altar of the king of Assyria in the temple, where the sacrificial altar stood.† In a

---

* Numbers 21:9.
† 4 Kings 16:11.

word, there is no evidence of any restriction on religion. I realize that most of the Jewish kings exterminated each other by
assassination, but that was because of their competing interests rather than their religious beliefs.

It is true that, among the prophets, there were some who
interceded with Heaven for revenge.* Elijah caused a fire to
descend from Heaven to consume the priests of Baal. Elisha
summoned bears to devour forty-two young children who had
called him bald. But these were rare miracles, which might be
a bit difficult if one wanted to imitate them.

People continue to object that the Jewish people were very
ignorant and barbarous. It is said† that when Moses was wag-
ing war with the Madianites,‡ he ordered all the male children
and mothers to be murdered and their spoils to be shared. The
conquerors found 675,000 sheep, 72,000 oxen, 61,000 asses
and 32,000 young women in the enemy camp. They shared
them among themselves and killed the rest. Some commentators even pretend that thirty-two girls were sacrificed to the
Lord: 'Out of the sixteen thousand persons, there fell to the
portion of the Lord, thirty-two souls.'8

In fact, the Jews did sacrifice human beings to the Divinity,
as is shown by the sacrifice of Jephthe§ or by that of king

---

* 3 Kings 18:38, 40; 4 Kings 2:24.
† Numbers 31.
‡ Madian was not included in the Promised Land. It is a small district in
Idumea, in Petrean Arabia, which extends from north of the River Arnon to
the River Zared, on the eastern shore of the Dead Sea. This land is inhabited
today by a small community of Arabs; it may be about eight leagues long and
a bit less wide. [Ed. The land in question was part of the Roman province of
Arabia that had Petra as its capital, which extended across the borders of
modern Jordan, Israel and the Sinai Peninsula. The River Arnon is mentioned
in Deuteronomy 2:24, and the River Zared is mentioned in Numbers 21:12.]
§ It is certain from the text that Jephthe sacrificed his daughter. 'God does
not approve of these vows,' says Dom Calmet in his dissertation on Jephthe's
vow, 'but when someone makes a vow, God wants it implemented, if for no
other reason than to punish those who make vows and to discourage the lev-
ity involved in making a vow without fearing that it must be implemented.'
St Augustine and nearly all the Fathers of the Church condemn Jephthe's
action. It is true that Scripture says that he was filled with the spirit of God

Agag,* who was cut into pieces by the priest Samuel. Even

---

and that St Paul, in his Epistle to the Hebrews, Chapter XI, praises Jephthe and places him in the company of Samuel and David.

St Jerome says, in his letter to Julian: 'Jephthe sacrificed his daughter to the Lord, and that is why the Apostle included him among the saints.' Those are the conflicting judgements about which we are not allowed to make any judgement ourselves. One should be afraid even to have an opinion on that issue. [*Ed.* Jephthe's vow to sacrifice the first person to come out of his house if God assisted him in battle is reported in Judges 11:31. The reference to St Paul is to Hebrews 11:32. Jerome's letter in Letter 118.]

* The death of the king Agag may be regarded as a genuine sacrifice. Saul had made this king of the Amalekites a prisoner of war and had accepted him as a hostage; but the priest Samuel had ordered him to spare nothing. He said to him, in these words: 'Kill everything, men and women, even young children and those who are still at their mother's breast.' 'Samuel cut the king Agag into pieces before the Lord, at Galgal.' 'The zeal that motivated the prophet,' says Dom Calmet, 'put a sword in his hand on this occasion to avenge the glory of the Lord and to confound Saul.' In this fatal incident, there was a dedication, a priest and a victim – it was therefore a sacrifice.

All the peoples of whom we have histories, except the Chinese, sacrificed human beings to the Divinity. Plutarch reports that even the Romans sacrificed human beings since the time of the Republic.

One finds in the *Commentaries* of Caesar that the Germans were about to sacrifice the hostages that Caesar had given them, when he rescued them by claiming victory.

I mentioned elsewhere that this violation of the law of nations in relation to Caesar's hostages, and the human victims who were sacrificed at the hands of women to increase the horror of the crime, undermines to some extent the panegyric about the Germans that Tacitus delivers in his treatise entitled *The Morals of the Germans*. It seems that, in his treatise, Tacitus is thinking more about satirizing the Romans than praising the Germans, about whom he knew very little.

Let us say here in passing that Tacitus loved satire more than truth. He wanted to make everything appear odious, even actions that were morally neutral, and we find his malice almost as pleasant as his style, because we enjoy malicious gossip and wit.

Let us return to the human victims. Our own forefathers sacrificed them just as much as the Germans. It is the ultimate expression of the stupidity of our human nature when left to its own resources, and it is one of the results of the weakness of our judgement. We think: we must offer what is most precious and most beautiful to God. We have nothing more beautiful than our own children. We must therefore choose the youngest and most beautiful among them to sacrifice to the Divinity.

Ezechiel promised them* that they would eat human flesh. 'You shall eat,' he said, 'horses and their riders; you shall drink the blood of princes.' Many commentators apply two verses of this prophet to the Jews themselves and the other verses to carnivorous animals. In the whole history of this people there is no sign of generosity, magnanimity or beneficence. But some rays of toleration always break through the fog of this long, appalling barbarity.

Jephthe, who was inspired by God and to whom he had sacrificed his only daughter, said to the Amorrhites:† 'Do you not have a right to what your god Chamos gave you? Allow us, therefore, to seize the land that our God promised us.' That is a specific declaration that may imply many things; but it is at least a compelling proof that God tolerated Chamos. The Holy Scripture does not say: 'You think you have a right to the lands that you claim were given to you by the god Chamos.' It says, in a positive way: 'You have a right (*tibi jure debentur*)'; that is the true meaning of the Hebrew words 'Ôtô tîrasch'.⁹

The story about Michas and the Levite, which is reported in Chapters 17 and 18 of the Book of Judges, is another incontrovertible proof that the Jews allowed the greatest possible

---

Philo says that, in the land of Canaan, they sacrificed their children to God on a number of occasions before God had ordered Abraham to sacrifice his only son to demonstrate his faith in God.

Sanchuniathon, who is cited by Eusebius, reports that the Phoenicians sacrificed their most precious children during periods of great danger, and that Ilus sacrificed his son Jephod at about the same time as God tested the faith of Abraham. It is difficult to see through the clouds of antiquity. But it is unfortunately true that these horrible sacrifices were practised almost everywhere. Nations gave up that practice only gradually as they became civilized; decency brings humanity in its wake.

[*Ed.* The story about Agag is in 1 Samuel (1 Kings) 15. Plutarch, *Roman Questions*, 83, questioned why the Romans blamed the Bletonesii for having sacrificed a man to the gods, when they had buried alive two men and two women in the cattle market, two of whom were Greeks and two were Gauls. Caesar's *Commentaries* on the Gallic war report the story of the rescue of the hostages. Philo Judæus (Philo of Alexandria) (*c.* 30 BC–*c.* AD 40) was the source of this story about sacrificing children. Eusebius, *Praeparatio Evangelica* {The Preparation for the Gospel}, Bk IV, Ch. 16, reports the story about Sanchuniathon.]

* Ezechiel 39:18.

† Judges 11:24.

liberty and toleration at that time. Michas's mother, a rich woman from Ephraim, had lost 1,100 silver coins. Her son returned them to her. She vowed to offer this money to the Lord, and she had it made into idols and built a small chapel. A Levite served in the chapel in exchange for an annual payment of ten silver coins, a tunic, an overcoat and his food. And Michas cried out:* 'Now I know that God will be good to me, because I have a priest from the Levite nation in my home.'

Meanwhile 600 men of the tribe of Dan, who were looking for a village in the countryside that they could seize and in which they could establish a settlement, did not have any Levite priest in their company, although they needed one so that God would support their expedition. They therefore went to Michas and took his ephod, his idols and his Levite priest, despite the objections of the priest and those of Michas and his mother. They then set off confidently to attack the village called Lais, and burned everything in it and killed all its inhabitants in accordance with their custom. They renamed the village 'Dan' to commemorate their victory. They placed Michas's idol on an altar; and, what is much more surprising, Jonathan, the grandson of Moses, was the high priest of this temple where they adored the God of Israel and Michas's idol.

After the death of Gideon, the Hebrews worshipped Baal for almost twenty years and gave up the cult of God without any leader, judge or priest seeking vengeance. I admit that this was a great crime, but if even this idolatry was tolerated, how must they have tolerated mere differences in the celebration of the true cult?

Some people offer the following as proof of intolerance. When the Lord had allowed His Ark of the Covenant to be captured by the Philistines in a battle, He punished the Philistines only by inflicting on them a hidden illness that resembled haemorrhoids, by overturning the statue of Dagon and by sending a plague of rats into their fields. But when the Philistines, in an attempt to appease His anger, returned the Ark yoked to two cows that were feeding their calves and offered God five golden rats and five golden anuses, the Lord had

* Judges 17:13.

seventy elders of Israel and 50,000 of the people of Israel killed because they had looked at the Ark. In response to that argument, however, one may reply that the Lord's punishment was not directed at a belief or a difference in religious practice or an instance of idolatry.[10]

If the Lord had wished to punish idolatry He would have killed all the Philistines who dared to look at the Ark and who had adored Dagon. But He killed 50,070 men of His own people only because they had looked at His Ark, which was something they ought not to have done. That shows how much the laws, the customs of the period and the Jewish economy differed from anything that we are familiar with today. It shows how much the inscrutable ways of God transcend our own. 'The severity applied to this large number of men,' says the judicious Dom Calmet, 'would appear excessive only to those who do not understand the extent to which God wanted to be feared and respected by His people, and who judge God's understanding and intentions by using the feeble light of their own reason.'[11]

God, therefore, did not punish a strange religious practice, but something that He considered to be a profanation of the worship that was due to Him, an indiscreet curiosity, a case of disobedience and perhaps even a rebellious attitude. It is evident that God used these kinds of punishment only in the Jewish theocracy. One cannot repeat often enough that those customs and times were completely different from ours.

Finally, during subsequent centuries, when the idolatrous Naaman asked Elisha if he was allowed to follow his king into the temple of Remmon and 'to adore with him there', did the same Elisha – who had had children devoured by bears – not reply to him: 'Go in peace'?*

There was much more than that. The Lord commanded Jeremiah† to put ropes around his neck, to wear collars and

---

* 4 Kings 20:25 [*Ed*. The correct reference is 4 Kings (2 Kings) 5:19.]
† Those who are not familiar with ancient customs and who judge matters only by what is familiar to them may be surprised by these strange events. But one must remember that, at that time in Egypt and a large part of Asia, most things were expressed in symbols, hieroglyphs, signs and examples.

The prophets, who called themselves seers among the Egyptians and Jews, not only expressed themselves in allegories but they represented the events that they foretold by using symbols. Thus Isaiah, the first of the four great Jewish prophets, took a scroll and wrote on it: '*chash baz*, gather quickly.' Then he lay with the prophetess; she became pregnant and gave birth to a son whom she named 'Hasten' [Isaiah 8:3]. That was a sign of the harms that Egypt and Assyria would cause the Jews.

This prophet said: 'Before this child is old enough to eat butter and honey or knows to choose good and avoid evil, the land that you detested will be delivered from two kings, the Lord will whistle at the flies of Egypt and the bees of Assyria, the Lord will take a borrowed razor and will shave off the beard and the hair of the feet from the king of Assyria' [Isaiah 7:15–20].

This prophecy about bees and about shaving off a beard and hair of the feet can be understood only by those who know that it was customary to call swarms by using the sound of a flute or some other rural instrument; that the worst insult a man could suffer was to have his beard shaved off; that the phrase 'hair of the feet' was used to refer to pubic hair, and that it was shaved off only when someone had some revolting disease such as leprosy. All these figures of speech, which are so foreign to the way we speak, mean only that the Lord would deliver His people from bondage within a few years.

The same Isaiah (Isaiah 20) walked about completely naked, to show that the king of Assyria would lead a group of captives who did not have enough clothes to cover their nakedness out of Egypt and Ethiopia.

Ezechiel (Ezechiel 4 ff) eats the roll of parchment that is presented to him. Then he covers his bread with excrement, and remains asleep on his left side for 390 days and on his right side for forty days, to mean that the Jews would lack bread, and to signify the number of years that their captivity would last. He loads himself with chains, which symbolize the chains of his people; he cuts his hair and beard and divides them into three parts. The first third signifies those who would perish in the city; the second, those who would be put to death around the city walls; and the third, those who would be led to Babylon.

The prophet Hosea (Hosea 3) married an adulterous woman, whom he bought with fifteen silver coins and one and a half bushels of barley. 'You will wait for me,' he told her, 'for many days, and during that time no man will approach you. That is the condition in which the children of Israel, for a long time, will be without a king, a prince, a sacrifice, an altar or an ephod.' In a word, the nabi, the seers, the prophets, almost never predict anything without using some sign to signify the predicted event.

Jeremiah, therefore, merely conforms to this custom when he binds himself with ropes, wears collars and puts yokes on his back, to signify the slavery of those to whom he gives these symbolic messages. If one wishes to read these texts carefully, one must realize that they belong to a period in an ancient world that is completely different to the new world: civil life, laws, the way war is waged, religious ceremonies – everything is absolutely different. One only has to open Homer or the first book of Herodotus to be

yokes, and to send them to the kings or *melakim* of Moab, Ammon, Edom, Tyre and Sidon: and the Lord had Jeremiah say to them: 'I have given all your lands to Nabuchodonosor, the king of Babylonia, who is my servant.'* Here is an idolatrous king who is declared to be God's servant and favourite.

The same Jeremiah, whom the Jewish king or *melek* named Zedekiah had thrown into a dungeon and subsequently pardoned, advised him on behalf of God to surrender to the king of Babylonia.† 'If you go and surrender to his officers,' he said, 'your soul will live.' God therefore finally takes sides with an idolatrous king. He gives over the Ark to him, the very sight of which had cost the lives of 50,070 Jews. He gives him the holy of holies and the rest of the temple, the construction of which had cost 108,000 gold talents, 1,017,000 silver talents, and 10,000 gold drachmas, which had been donated by David and his officers for building the house of the Lord. Without

---

convinced that we are not in any way like the prophets of early antiquity and that we should distrust our judgement when we try to compare their customs with ours.

Even nature was not the same then as now. Magicians had a power over nature then that they no longer have; they cast spells on snakes, they recalled the dead, etc. God sent dreams and men interpreted them. The gift of prophecy was common. There were examples of metamorphosis such as Nabuchodonosor being changed into a bullock, Lot's wife being changed into a statue of salt, and five towns that changed into a burning lake.

In those days there were certain kinds of human beings who no longer exist either. The race of giants called Rephaim, Enim, Nephilim and Anakim has disappeared. St Augustine says, in Book V of *The City of God* [*Ed*. Bk. XV, Ch. 9], that he saw the tooth of an ancient giant that was as large as one hundred of our molars. Ezechiel speaks of the Gammidim pygmies, who were only as high as our elbow and who fought at the siege of Tyre [Ezechiel 27:11]. In almost all these stories, the sacred authors of Scripture agree with secular authors. The illnesses and cures were not the same then as in our day. Those who were possessed were cured with a root called *baaras*, which was attached to a ring on the end of one's nose.

Finally, the whole ancient world was so different to ours that one cannot infer any rule of conduct from it. And even if peoples persecuted or oppressed each other because of their religious beliefs in this remote antiquity, we should not imitate that kind of cruelty in the new dispensation of the law of grace.

* Jeremiah 27:6.
† Jeremiah 27:12.

counting the money spent by Solomon, that comes to a total of approximately 19,062 million in today's currency. Idolatry was never rewarded so well. I know that this calculation is exaggerated and that it probably includes some mistake by a copyist; but if you reduce it to half the total, or to a quarter or even an eighth, it is still surprising. The riches that Herodotus said he had seen in the temple of Ephesus are hardly less surprising.[12] Of course, treasures are nothing in the eyes of God, and the title of 'servant' – which was given to Nabuchodonosor – is the real treasure of inestimable value.

God does not show any less favour to Kir or Koresh or Kosroes, whom we call Cyrus.* He calls him His Christ, His anointed, although he was not anointed in the usual sense of that term and followed the religion of Zoroaster. He calls him His shepherd, although in the eyes of the world he was a usurper. There is no greater sign of predilection in the whole of sacred Scripture.

You see in Malachi that 'from the rising to the setting of the Sun, God's name is great among the nations, and everywhere they offer him pure oblations.'[13] God takes care of the idolatrous Ninevites just as much as the Jews; he threatens them and pardons them. Melchisedeck, who was not Jewish, offered a sacrifice to God. Balaam, an idolater, was a prophet. Scripture thus teaches us that, not only does God tolerate all other peoples, but He also extends to them His paternal care. And we dare to be intolerant!

* Isaiah 44, 45.

THIRTEEN

The Extraordinary Toleration
of the Jews

Thus you always see examples of toleration under Moses, in
the time of the judges and the time of the kings. There is even
much more than that. Moses says a number of times that 'God
punishes fathers through their children, up to the fourth
generation.'* This threat was necessary for a people to whom
God had not revealed either the immortality of the soul or the
punishment or rewards of the afterlife. He did not reveal these
truths to them in the Decalogue or in any law in Leviticus or
Deuteronomy. These were doctrines that were known among
the Persians, Babylonians, Egyptians, Greeks and Cretans, but
they were not part of the Jewish religion. Moses did not say:
'Honour thy father and thy mother, if you wish to go to Heaven',
but he said: 'Honour thy father and mother . . . that thou mayst
live a long time, and it may be well with thee in the land.'[1] He
threatened them with only corporal punishments – scabies,
boils and ulcers on the knee and calf; the infidelity of their
wives; having to borrow from strangers and paying them interest without being able to lend to others with interest; dying
of famine and being forced to eat their own children.† But
nowhere does God say to them that their immortal souls would
suffer torments after death or that they would enjoy the happiness of Heaven. God, who led His people Himself, punished or
rewarded them immediately after they had done something
good or bad. Everything was temporal, and that is a truth that
Warburton[2] exploits to prove that Jewish law was divine: since

* Exodus 20:5.
† Deuteronomy 28.

God Himself was their king,* who dispensed justice immediately after any transgression or disobedience, He did not need to reveal to them a doctrine that He withheld until a later time when He no longer governed His people. Those who ignorantly think that Moses taught the immortality of the soul deprive the New Testament of one of the features by which it greatly surpasses the Old Testament. It is clear that the law of Moses

* There is only one passage in the law of Moses from which one could conclude that Moses was informed about the belief that the soul does not die with the body, which was something that was commonly believed among the Egyptians. That passage is very important and is found in Deuteronomy 18 (vv. 10–11): 'Do not consult soothsayers who predict future events by looking at the clouds, who cast spells on snakes, who consult the soul of Python, seers or wise men who question the dead and ask them to tell the truth.'

This passage seems to suggest that if one called upon the souls of the dead, the so-called spell presupposed that souls continued to live after death. It is also possible, however, that the magicians that Moses spoke about were merely great deceivers and that they had no clear understanding of the spell that they thought they were casting. They got people to believe that they forced the dead to speak and that, by their magic, they restored them to the condition in which their bodies had been when they were alive, without considering at all whether one could or could not infer the doctrine of the soul's immortality from their ridiculous machinations. The sorcerers were never philosophers; they were always stupid jugglers who performed for imbeciles.

It is also noticeable that the word 'Python' is used in Deuteronomy a long time before this Greek word could have been known to the Jews. Besides, the word 'Python' is not a Hebrew word, so that we do not know exactly what it means when used there.

There are insurmountable difficulties in the Hebrew language. It is a mixture of Phoenician, Egyptian, Syriac and Arabic, and this ancient mixture has been modified very much since then. Hebrew verbs never had more than two tenses, the present and the future; other tenses had to be inferred from the context. Different vowels were often written by using the same characters or, in fact, they did not write the vowels at all and those who invented points only made matters worse. Every adverb has twenty different meanings. The same word may be understood in completely different ways.

Add to this confusion the limitations and poverty of language in general. The Jews, who lacked the relevant arts, were unable to express what they did not know. In a word, Hebrew is to Greek what a peasant language is to that of a member of the Académie française. [Ed. Voltaire's argument about the word 'Python' is mistaken, since there is no such word in Deuteronomy 18:11 in the Hebrew text. The Vulgate uses the term *pythones* in the plural, which translated a Hebrew word that probably meant a familiar spirit or medium, which would be consistent with the context of divination.]

announced only temporal punishments up to the fourth generation. Nonetheless, despite the clear promulgation of this law and despite God's explicit threat that He would punish up to the fourth generation, Ezechiel announced the exact opposite to the Jews and told them that a son would not bear the iniquity of his father.* He even went so far as to have God say† that He had given them 'commandments that were not good'.‡

The Book of Ezechiel was accepted, nonetheless, among the canonical authors that had been inspired by God. It is true that the Synagogue did not allow people under the age of thirty to read it, as St Jerome tells us,[3] but that was because they feared that young people would be corrupted by the extremely vivid portraits of the licentious behaviour of the two sisters Oolla and Ooliba, in Chapters 16 and 23. In summary, Ezechiel's book was always recognized as canonical despite being formally inconsistent with Moses.[4]

Finally,§ when the doctrine of the immortality of the soul was adopted, which probably began about the same time as

---

* Ezechiel 18:20.

† Ezechiel 20:25.

‡ Ezechiel's opinion eventually prevailed in the synagogue. But there were Jews who believed in eternal punishments and consequently that God pursued the iniquities of fathers in their children. Today they are punished beyond the fiftieth generation while they also have to fear eternal punishments. One wonders about the descendants of those Jews who were not complicit in the death of Jesus Christ – those who lived in Jerusalem but had no part in his death, and those who were dispersed throughout the rest of the world – how could they suffer temporal punishments in their children, who were just as innocent as their fathers? This temporal punishment or rather this way of living that differs from that of other peoples and of being involved in business without having a fatherland, cannot be considered a punishment at all when compared with the eternal punishment that results from their incredulity, which they could avoid by means of a sincere conversion.

§ Those who wished to find the doctrine about Hell and Paradise (as we understand it) in the Pentateuch are strangely mistaken. Their error results from a silly dispute about words. When the Vulgate translated the Hebrew word *sheol* ('tomb') by the Latin word *infernum*, and the Latin term was then translated by the French word *enfer* (Hell), they relied on this equivocation to persuade people that the ancient Hebrews had the same concept that the Greeks call Hades and Tartarus, and which other nations had known previously by different names.

It is reported in Chapter 16 of the Book of Numbers [16:31–3] that the earth opened its mouth beneath the tents of Core, Dathan and Abiron, that the earth devoured them together with their tents and possessions and that they were thrown alive into an underground sepulchre. There is certainly no mention in this text of the souls of the three Hebrews or of the torments of Hell or eternal punishments.

It is strange that in the *Encyclopedia Dictionary*, in the article on 'Hell', it is said that the ancient Hebrews 'had recognized its reality'. If that were the case, it would constitute an unacceptable contradiction in the Pentateuch. How could Moses have spoken in a single isolated passage about punishments after death when he never mentioned them in his laws? The thirty-second chapter of Deuteronomy is quoted, but it is abbreviated. Here is the full text: 'They have provoked me with that which was no god, and have angered me with their vanities: and I will provoke them with that which is no people, and will vex them with a foolish nation. A fire is kindled in my wrath, and shall burn even to the lowest Hell: and shall devour the earth with her increase, and shall burn the foundations of the mountains. I will heap evils upon them, and will spend my arrows among them. They shall be consumed with famine, and birds shall devour them with a most bitter bite: I will send the teeth of beasts upon them, with the fury of creatures that trail upon the ground, and of serpents.'

Is there the slightest connection between these verses and the idea of eternal punishments as we understand them? It seems rather that these words were reported only to make us see that Hell, as we understand it, was unknown among the ancient Jews.

The author of this article also cites (p. 665) the passage from the Book of Job, Chapter 24: 'The eye of the adulterer observeth darkness, saying: No eye shall see me: and he will cover his face. He diggeth through houses in the dark, as in the day they had appointed for themselves, and they have not known the light. If the morning suddenly appear, it is to them the shadow of death: and they walk in darkness as if it were in light. He is light upon the face of the water: cursed be his portion on the earth, let him not walk by the way of the vineyards. Let him pass from the snow waters to excessive heat, and his sin even to Hell.' Or perhaps 'the grave has dissipated those who sin' or possibly (according to the Septuagint Bible) 'their sin was recalled in their memory'.

I quote these passages in their entirety, and literally, for otherwise it is impossible to get an accurate idea of them.

Is there the slightest word there, I ask you, from which one could conclude that Moses taught the Jews the clear and simple doctrine of punishments and rewards after death?

The Book of Job has no connection with the laws of Moses. Besides, it is very likely that Job was not Jewish; that is the opinion of St Jerome in his Hebrew questions about the Book of Genesis. The word 'Satan' which occurs in Job was unknown to the Jews, and it is not found anywhere in the Pentateuch. The Jews learned this word only in Chaldea, just like the names Gabriel and Raphael, which were unknown before their slavery in Babylonia. It is therefore very inappropriate to cite Job in this context.

the Babylonian captivity, the sect of the Sadducees continued

---

They also refer to the last chapter of Isaiah: 'And there shall be month after month, and sabbath after sabbath: and all flesh shall come to adore before my face, saith the Lord. And they shall go out, and see the carcasses of the men that have transgressed against me by the roadside: their worm shall not die, and their fire shall not be quenched: and they shall be a loathsome sight to all flesh' [Isaiah 66:23–4].

Certainly, if they are thrown onto the side of the road, if they are exposed to the view of all passers-by, and if they are consumed by worms that does not mean that Moses taught the Jews the dogma of the immortality of the soul. And these words 'their fire shall not be quenched' do not mean that the carcasses that are exposed to public view would undergo the eternal punishments of Hell.

How could one quote a passage from Isaiah to prove that the Jews who lived at the time of Moses had been taught the dogma of the soul's immortality? Isaiah prophesied, according to the Hebrew computation, during the year 3380 in the history of the world. Moses lived about the year 2500. Eight centuries passed between one and the other. It is an insult to common sense or just a joke to abuse one's freedom to quote in this way, and to claim to prove that one author had held a certain opinion by citing a passage by another author who came eight centuries later and who had never mentioned that particular opinion. It is indubitable that the immortality of the soul, and punishments and rewards after death, were announced, recognized and established in the New Testament and it is indubitable that they are not found anywhere in the Pentateuch. That is what the great Arnauld said clearly and with conviction in his defence of Port-Royal.

The Jews, when they believed since then [i.e., after the New Testament] in the immortality of the soul, were not clear about its spirituality; they thought, just like almost all other nations, that the soul was something light, made of air, a flimsy substance, which retained some resemblance to the body that it animated. It is what was called the 'shades' or the 'manes of bodies'. That was the opinion of many Fathers of the Church. Tertullian, in Chapter 22 of *The Soul*, writes as follows: 'We define the soul as a simple, immortal, corporeal and substantial image, which is born from the breath of God.'

St Irenaeus says in Book II, Ch. 34: 'Souls are incorporeal in comparison with mortal bodies.' He adds that 'Jesus Christ taught that souls preserve the images of bodies in which they are embodied, etc.' There is no indication that Jesus Christ ever taught that doctrine and it is difficult to know what St Irenaeus means.

St Hilary is more formal and positive in his commentary on the Gospel according to Matthew, where he clearly attributes a corporeal substance to the soul: 'They are assigned the corporeal substance of their nature.'

St Ambrose, on Abraham, Book II, Ch. 8, claims that nothing is completely immaterial apart from the substance of the Holy Trinity.

One might reproach these honourable men for holding a mistaken philosophy. But we should believe that their theology was fundamentally very wise, to believe that there was neither reward nor punishment after death, and that the faculty of sensation and thought perishes when someone dies, together with their active powers, such as their ability to walk and to digest food. They denied the

---

because, without knowing the incomprehensible nature of the soul, they confirmed that it is immortal and wanted it to be Christian.

We know that the soul is spiritual, but we do not know at all what is meant by 'spiritual'. We know matter very imperfectly and we find it impossible to conceive a distinct idea of what is not material. Since we are very poorly informed about what affects our senses, we are incapable of knowing anything about what is beyond our senses if we rely on our own natural abilities. We transfer some words from our ordinary language into the depths of metaphysics and theology to provide some idea of things that we can neither conceive nor express. We try to prop ourselves up with these words to support, if possible, our feeble understanding in areas where we know nothing.

Thus we use the word 'spirit', which corresponds to 'breath' and 'wind', to describe something that is not matter. And since these words 'spirit', 'breath' and 'wind' lead us in spite of ourselves to the idea of a delicate or light substance, we subtract whatever we can from that substance to get to a point where we conceive of pure spirituality. But we never succeed in acquiring a distinct concept; we do not even know what we are saying when we pronounce the word 'substance'. Literally it means whatever is underneath, and that alone tells us that it is incomprehensible. For what in fact is meant by 'whatever is underneath'? Our knowledge does not extend to sharing in God's secrets in this life. Since we are plunged into deep shadows, we bump into each other and we beat about aimlessly in the midst of this darkness without knowing precisely why we are making the effort.

If one reflects carefully on all that, no reasonable person will fail to conclude that we should be tolerant of other people's opinions and should respect them.

All these comments are relevant to the fundamental question whether human beings should tolerate each other. For if they show how much people have been mistaken about different things from time immemorial, they also show that human beings ought to have treated each other with indulgence at all times. [*Ed.* Voltaire translates *sheol* as a tomb or grave, but the Hebrew term meant something more like 'the underworld' or 'the abode of the dead'. He claims to quote literally from the Book of Job, although he provides his own French translation of the Vulgate rather than that of Lemaistre de Sacy. The reference to St Jerome is to his *Hebraicae quaestiones in libro Geneseos* {Hebrew Questions on the Book of Genesis}. Voltaire's comments on the word *Satan* as used in Job 1-2 are unreliable, because the Hebrew term *ha-satan* meant 'the adversary' – someone who was an adversary of God, rather than a proper name for a particular fallen angel. Antoine Arnauld, together with Pierre Nicole and Claude de Sainte-Marthe, wrote a defence of Port-Royal in *Apologie pour les religieuses de Port-Royal* {A Defence of the Religious Sisters of Port-Royal}. The quotation from St Irenaeus is from his *Adversus Haereses* {Against Heresies}.]

existence of angels. They differed from other Jews in their beliefs more than Protestants differ from Catholics, but they did not cease, for that reason, to remain in communion with their brothers. There were even great priests among the members of their sect.

The Pharisees believed in fate* and the transmigration of souls.† The Essenes believed that the souls of the just went to the Isles of the Blessed,‡ while the souls of the wicked went to

---

* The doctrine about fate is both ancient and universal. You find it throughout Homer. Jupiter wished to save the life of his son Sarpedon, but fate had condemned him to death and Jupiter had to obey. The philosophers understood destiny either as the necessary connection of causes with effects that were necessarily produced by nature, or this same connection as ordained by Providence (which is more reasonable). This whole system of fate is contained in the following verse of Seneca: 'Fate leads those who are willing, and tugs those who are unwilling.'

It has always been accepted that God governs the universe by eternal, universal and immutable laws. This truth was the source of all the unintelligible disputes about freedom, because no one had ever defined freedom before the wise Locke arrived. He proved that freedom is the power to act. God gives this power; and human beings, while acting freely in accordance with the eternal commands of God, are wheels within the great machine of the world. The whole of antiquity disputed about freedom, but no one persecuted others on account of their disputes until now. What an absurd horror to have imprisoned and exiled Arnauld d'Andilly, Antoine Arnauld, a Sacy, a Nicole, and so many others who were the light of France! [Ed. Homer, Iliad, Book XVI tells the story of the death of Jupiter's son Sarpedon. The lines from Seneca are from the Moral Letters to Lucilius, Letter 107. The final lines of Voltaire's note refer to some of the prominent supporters of Jansenism in the seventeenth century when the Church and Louis XIV closed and demolished the Jansenist convent at Port-Royal des Champs. They include Robert Arnauld d'Andilly (1589–1674), Antoine Arnauld (1612–94), Louis-Isaac Le Maistre de Sacy (1613–84), whose French translation of the Bible Voltaire consulted, and Pierre Nicole (1625–95), the author with Antoine Arnauld of Logic or the Art of Thinking (1662).]

† The theological story about the transmigration of souls comes from India, from which we have inherited many more fables than is commonly assumed. This doctrine is explained in the admirable fifteenth book of Ovid's Metamorphoses; it was accepted almost everywhere in the world, and it was also always opposed. But we do not see that any priest in antiquity ever imprisoned one of Pythagoras's followers.

‡ Neither the ancient Jews, nor the Egyptians, nor their contemporary Greeks believed that human souls went to Heaven after death. The Jews thought that the Sun and Moon were a few leagues above us, in the same

some kind of Tartarus. They did not offer sacrifices and assembled among themselves in a separate synagogue. In brief, if Judaism is examined closely, it surprisingly reveals the greatest level of toleration combined with the most barbarous horrors. That is truly a contradiction, but nearly all peoples were subject to contradictions. It would be a happy people indeed whose customs are gentle when their laws are written in blood!

---

sphere, and that the firmament was a thick and solid vault that supported the weight of the waters, which escaped through some apertures. The palace of the gods, according to the ancient Greeks, was on Mount Olympus. In Homer's time the abode of heroes after death was on an island beyond the ocean, and that was also what the Essenes believed.

Since the time of Homer, planets were assigned to different gods, but men had no more reason to place a god on the Moon than the inhabitants of the Moon had reason to place a god on Earth. Juno and Iris had only the clouds as a palace and they had nowhere there to rest their feet. According to the Sabaeans, each god had their own star. But since a star was a sun, it was impossible to live there unless one had the same nature as fire. Therefore, to ask what the ancients thought about Heaven is a completely useless question. The best reply is that they did not think about it at all.

FOURTEEN

Did Jesus Christ Teach Intolerance?

Let us now see if Jesus Christ established any bloodthirsty laws, if he commanded people to be intolerant, if he built dungeons for an Inquisition or instituted executioners who would burn people at the stake for their beliefs.

If I am not mistaken, there are very few passages in the Gospels from which someone who is disposed to persecute others could conclude that intolerance and enforced belief are legitimate. One such passage is the parable in which the kingdom of Heaven is compared with a king who invites guests to the wedding celebration of his son. This monarch has his servants tell the guests: 'my oxen and fatlings are killed, and all things are ready. Come ye to the marriage.'* Some of them ignore the invitation and go to their houses in the country, while others take care of their business; others again insult the king's servants and kill them. The king sends his army against those murderers and destroys their town. He sends out his servants into the main roads to invite everyone they meet to the wedding. One of those who comes to the feast without an appropriate wedding garment is bound in chains and cast out into the exterior darkness.

It is clear that this allegory applies only to the kingdom of Heaven. Certainly, no one should conclude from it that it gives them a right to strangle or imprison their neighbour who happens to come to dinner at their home without an appropriate wedding garment, and I know of no ruler in history who had a courtier hanged in those circumstances. Nor should we fear, if

* Matthew 22:4.

an emperor prepares fowl and sends his servants to the princes
of the Empire to invite them to dinner, that the princes would
kill the servants. The invitation to the festivities signifies
preaching about salvation. The murder of the king's servants
symbolizes the persecution of those who preach wisdom and
virtue.

The other parable* is about an individual who invites his
friends to a great dinner and, when he is ready to sit down and
dine, he sends his servant to alert them. One of the guests
excused himself because he had bought some land and wanted
to visit it. That excuse does not seem valid because no one
inspects their land during the night. Another guest said that he
had bought five pairs of oxen and that he wanted to test them.
He was just as wrong as the previous guest, because dinner-
time is not the time for testing oxen. A third guest replied that
he had just got married and his excuse is certainly acceptable.
The father of the family was angry and got the blind and crip-
pled to come to his feast and, when he saw that there were still
some empty seats at the table, he said to his servant: 'Go out
into the highways and hedges, and compel them to come in,
that my house may be filled.'

It is true that this parable is not explicitly said to be a symbol of the kingdom of Heaven. These words 'compel them to
come in' have been very much abused.[1] But it is obvious that
one servant alone could not possibly force everyone he encoun-
ters on the main roads to come and dine with his master.
Besides, guests who are forced in that way would not make the
dinner very enjoyable. According to the most reliable commentators, 'compel them to come in' means only the following:
ask, implore, entice or succeed. What possible connection, I
ask, could this invitation to dinner have with persecution?

If one reads the parable literally, would someone have to be
blind, lame and led by force in order to belong in the bosom of
the Church? Jesus says in the same parable: 'Do not give dinner
to your friends or your rich relatives.' Has anyone ever

* Luke 14:16.

concluded that they should not dine with their relatives or their friends once they become moderately wealthy?

Jesus Christ, after the Parable of the Feast, says:* 'If any man come to me, and hate not his father and mother and wife and children and brethren and sisters, yea and his own life also, he cannot be my disciple, etc. For which of you, having a mind to build a tower, doth not first sit down and reckon the charges that are necessary?' Is there anyone in the world who is so unnatural as to conclude that they should hate their father and mother? Is it not easy to understand that these words mean the following: Do not compare me with those who are dearest to you.

There is a passage from St Matthew that is also quoted:† 'And if he will not hear the church, let him be to thee as the heathen and publican.' That certainly does not mean that one should persecute pagans and those who gather taxes on behalf of the Crown. It is true that they are cursed, but they are not handed over to the civil powers. Far from depriving tax-gatherers of any prerogatives of a citizen, they were accorded the highest privileges. That is the only profession that is condemned in Scripture and is the one most valued by governments. Why then could we not tolerate our errant brothers as much as we lavish consideration on our brothers who collect taxes?

Another passage that has been grossly abused is one from St Matthew and St Mark, where it says that Jesus approached a fig tree when he was hungry one morning and found that it had nothing but leaves, because it was not the season for figs. He cursed the fig tree and it immediately dried up.

Commentators offer different explanations of this miracle, but would any of them justify persecution? A fig tree could not have produced figs at the beginning of March and it was dried up. Is that a reason to shrivel our brothers with pain during the whole year? Let us respect whatever we find in Scripture that

* Luke 14:26 ff.
† Matthew 18:17.

may challenge our curious and vain minds, but let us not abuse it to justify becoming hard and implacable.

The spirit of persecution, which abuses everything, continues to look for an excuse in the expulsion of the merchants who were thrown out of the temple and in the legion of devils that were expelled from the body of a possessed person into the bodies of 2,000 unclean animals.[2] But who could fail to see that these two episodes are merely examples of the justice that God deigns to apply to those who break the law? It was a lack of respect for the house of the Lord to convert the square outside the temple into a marketplace for merchants. The Sanhedrin and priests were wrong to allow this kind of market for the convenience of those who came to offer a sacrifice. The God to whom the sacrifices were offered – although hidden in human form – was certainly entitled to destroy that kind of profanation. He could also punish, by the same token, those who introduced into the country entire herds of animals that were forbidden by a law of which He Himself deigned to be the guardian. These examples have no connection whatsoever with persecuting people because of their religious beliefs. The spirit of intolerance must depend on rather poor reasons since it searches for the most inadequate pretexts all over the place.

Nearly all the other words and actions of Jesus Christ preach sweetness, patience and toleration. There is the father of a family who welcomes back his prodigal son; there is the labourer who arrives at the end of the day and is paid as much as the others; and there is also the Good Samaritan. Christ himself tells his disciples that they need not fast; he forgives the woman who sins; he is satisfied merely to advise an adulterous woman to be faithful; he even deigns to join in the innocent joy of the wedding guests at Cana who, having already drunk plenty of wine, asked for more. He was quite willing to work a miracle on their behalf and changed water into wine.[3]

He does not even get angry with Judas, who was about to betray him. He commands Peter never to use a sword; he reprimands the sons of Zebedee [James and John], who wished to follow the example of Elias by calling down fire from Heaven on a town that refused to provide them with lodging.[4]

Finally he died as a victim of envy. If one dared to compare the sacred and profane, to compare God with a human being, the death of Jesus Christ had a lot in common with that of Socrates when judged from a human point of view. The Greek philosopher perished because of the hatred of the sophists, priests and leaders of the people. The lawgiver for Christians succumbed to the hatred of the scribes, Pharisees and priests. Socrates could have avoided death, but he chose not to do so, while Jesus Christ offered himself voluntarily to death. The Greek philosopher not only forgave his accusers and iniquitous judges, but he asked them to treat his children as he was treated if they were fortunate enough, some day, to deserve the judges' hatred. The lawgiver for Christians, infinitely superior, asked his father to forgive his enemies.[5]

If Jesus Christ appeared to fear death, if the agony he suffered was so extreme that his perspiration was mixed with blood, which is a very rare and violent symptom, it is because he deigned to experience all the fragility of the human body that he had assumed. His body shook, but his soul was unshakeable. He taught us that genuine strength and true greatness consist in enduring the miseries to which our nature is subject. There is the greatest courage in embracing death at the same time as dreading it.

Socrates had treated the sophists as if they were ignorant and had convicted them of bad faith. Jesus, taking advantage of his divine rights, treated the scribes* and Pharisees as hypocrites, fools, blind people, evildoers, serpents and a race of vipers.

Socrates was not accused of trying to found a new sect; nor was Jesus Christ accused of wanting to do so.† It is reported that the high priests and the whole council looked for false evidence against Jesus to ensure his death.

Now if they looked for false evidence, they did not therefore accuse him of having preached publicly against the law. In fact he was subject to the law of Moses from his infancy until his

* Matthew 23.
† Matthew 26.

death. He was circumcised on the eighth day, just like all the other children. If he was later baptized in the River Jordan, that was consistent with a ceremony that was sacred to the Jews and to all the other peoples of the East. All those who, according to the law, were tainted cleansed themselves by baptism. That was how they consecrated priests; they immersed themselves in water on the feast of the solemn expiation, and proselytes were baptized in the same way.

Jesus observed all the detailed prescriptions of the law. He celebrated every Sabbath day and abstained from forbidden foods. He celebrated all the feasts and even, before his death, he had celebrated the Passover. He was not accused of any novel belief or of having celebrated any strange religious rite. Having been born a Jew, he lived his life constantly as a Jew.

Two witnesses who came forward accused him of having said* 'that he could destroy the temple and rebuild it again in three days'. Such a speech was completely incomprehensible to worldly Jews; but it was not an accusation of wanting to found a novel sect.

The high priest interrogated him and said to him: 'I adjure thee by the living God, that thou tell us if thou be the Christ the Son of God.'[6] We are not told what the high priest meant by 'Son of God'. That expression was used occasionally to mean someone who was just,† in the same way as the words 'son of Belial'[7] were used to signify an evil person. Ordinary

---

* Matthew 26:61.

† In fact, it was very difficult (if not impossible) for the Jews to understand the ineffable mystery of the Incarnation of the Son of God, of God Himself, without a special revelation. Genesis (Ch. 6) calls the sons of powerful people 'sons of God'. In a similar way, the very tall cedars were called the 'cedars of God'. Samuel says that 'a fear of God' fell on the people, which is to say a great fear. A great wind was 'a wind of God' and the sickness of Saul was called 'the melancholy of God'. Nonetheless, it seems as if the Jews understood literally that Jesus called himself the son of God in the usual sense of that term. But they considered that description as blasphemous, which is possibly another proof of their ignorance of the Incarnation, of God and of the Son of God, who was sent on this Earth for the salvation of humankind. [*Ed.* Voltaire's biblical references are to Psalm 79:11; 1 Samuel (1 Kings) 7:10; the illness attributed to Saul in 1 Samuel (1 Kings) 16:15 is called a *'malus Dei'* in the Vulgate.]

Jews had no idea of the sacred mystery of a Son of God, of God Himself coming on Earth.

Jesus replied to him: 'Thou hast said it. Nevertheless I say to you, hereafter you shall see the Son of man sitting on the right hand of the power of God and coming in the clouds of Heaven.'[8]

The outraged Sanhedrin regarded this reply as blasphemy. Since the Sanhedrin no longer had judicial power, they transferred Jesus to the Roman governor of the province and accused him falsely of disturbing public order, of having said that it was not necessary to pay taxes to Caesar, and in addition of claiming to be king of the Jews. There is, therefore, overwhelming evidence that he was accused of offences against the State.

When Pilate, the governor, learned that he came from Galilee, he sent him initially to Herod, who was tetrarch of Galilee. Herod believed that it was impossible that Jesus could have hoped to make himself a political leader and to claim royal status. He treated him with contempt and sent him back to Pilate, who had the despicable weakness to condemn him in order to pacify the crowd that had assembled against him. That was all the more reprehensible since he had already experienced a rebellion by the Jews, according to what we learn from Josephus.[9] Pilate did not have the same generosity that the governor Festus displayed later.[10]

I shall now ask whether toleration or intolerance is divinely ordained. If you wish to resemble Jesus Christ, you ought to be martyrs rather than executioners.

FIFTEEN
Witnesses against Intolerance[1]

It is impious to take away the freedom of human beings in religious matters and to prevent them from choosing a divinity. No human being, no god, would wish to be served under duress. (*Apology*, Ch. 24)[2]

If violence were used to defend the faith, the bishops would oppose it. (St Hilary, Book I)

An enforced religion is no religion at all. It is necessary to persuade people rather than force them. Religion cannot be commanded. (Lactantius, Book III)[3]

Attempting to persuade by force, beating and imprisoning people whom we have failed to convince by reason, is a detestable heresy. (St Athanasius, Book I)

There is nothing more inconsistent with religion than coercion. (St Justin Martyr, Book V)

St Augustine asked the question, before his controversy with the Donatists made him too severe: 'Shall we persecute those whom God tolerates?'

Let no one do any violence to the Jews. (Fourth Council of Toledo, Session 56)

Advise, but do not coerce. (Letters of St Bernard)

We do not claim to destroy errors by violence. (*Discourse of the Clergy of France to Louis XIII*)

We have always disapproved of measures of enforcement. (Assembly of the Clergy, 11 August 1560)

We know that faith results from persuasion and that it cannot be commanded. (Fléchier, Bishop of Nîmes, Letter 19)

We should not even use insulting language. (Bishop Du Bellai in a pastoral letter)

Remember that the illnesses of the soul are not cured by coercion or violence. (Cardinal Le Camus, *Pastoral Instruction*, 1688)

Grant civil toleration to everyone. (Fénelon, Archbishop of Cambrai, to the Duke of Burgundy)

The enforced practice of religion is a clear proof that the person responsible for it is an enemy of the truth. (Dirois, Doctor of the Sorbonne, Book 6, Ch. 4)

Violence is capable of creating hypocrites; it is impossible to persuade people by issuing threats everywhere. (Tillemont, *Ecclesiastical History*, Vol. 6)[4]

It seemed to us that it is in keeping with justice and right reason to follow the example of the early Church, which did not use violence to establish and spread religion. (*Remonstrance of the Parlement of Paris to Henry II*)

Experience teaches us that violence is more likely to exacerbate rather than cure an illness that originates in the mind, etc. (De Thou, *Letter of Dedication to Henry IV*)[5]

Faith is not inspired by strokes of a sword. (Cérisiers, *The Reigns of Henry IV and Louis XIII*)

It is a barbaric zeal that claims to implant religion in human hearts, as if conviction could result from coercion. (Boulainvilliers, *The Condition of France*)

The same thing applies in religion as in love; a command can do nothing and compulsion even less. There is nothing more independent than loving and believing. (Amelot de la Houssaye, on the *Letters of Cardinal d'Ossat*)

If Heaven has loved you enough to let you see the truth, it has bestowed a great favour on you. But should those who have inherited from their father hate those who have not done so? (Montesquieu, *The Spirit of the Laws*, Book 25)[6]

One could write a very large book that is composed entirely of similar passages. Our histories, discourses, sermons, books on morality and catechisms all breathe and all teach this sacred duty of toleration today. What fate or inconsistency could make us deny in practice a theory that we proclaim every day? Our actions belie our morality only because we believe that we will benefit in some way by doing the opposite of what we teach. But there is certainly no benefit in persecuting those who do not share our opinion and causing them to hate us. There is, therefore, once again an absurdity in intolerance. But one might object that those who are interested in constraining the conscience of others are not absurd. The following brief dialogue is addressed to them.

SIXTEEN

A Dialogue between a Dying Man and a Man in Good Health

When a citizen was dying in a provincial town, another man in good health came to insult him in his last hours, and said to him:

Wretch! I order you to think as I do immediately; sign this document, and confess that there are five propositions in a book that neither you nor I have ever read.[1] You must immediately adopt the opinion of Lanfranc against Berengarius,[2] and that of St Thomas against St Bonaventure.[3] You must agree with the Second Council of Nicaea against the Council of Frankfurt;[4] and explain to me right away how the words 'My Father is greater than me' mean precisely 'I am as great as Him.'[5]

Explain to me how the Father communicates everything to the Son except paternity or I am going to throw your body in the ditch. Your children will not inherit anything from you, your wife will be deprived of her dowry and your family will beg for food, which those who share my beliefs will refuse to give them.

THE DYING MAN: I hardly understand what you are saying to me. I hear your threats in a rather confusing way; they disturb my soul and make my death dreadful. In the name of God, have pity on me!

THE BARBARIAN: You ask for pity! I cannot have pity on you unless you agree with everything that I believe.

THE DYING MAN: Alas! You know that, in these last few moments, all my senses are fading, all the doors of my understanding are closed, my ideas are vanishing and my thought is closing down. Am I in any condition to dispute with you?

THE BARBARIAN: Very well! If you are unable to believe what I want you to believe, at least say you believe it and that will satisfy me.

THE DYING MAN: How can I perjure myself just to please you? In a few minutes I am going to appear before God, who punishes those who commit perjury.

THE BARBARIAN: That doesn't matter. You will have the pleasure of being buried in a consecrated cemetery and your wife and children will have enough to live on. So die a hypocrite; hypocrisy is a good thing. As they say, it is the homage that vice pays to virtue.[6] A little hypocrisy, my friend, would cost you almost nothing.

THE DYING MAN: Alas! You either despise God or you do not acknowledge Him, because you are asking me to lie just as I am about to die, though you will soon be judged by Him and will have to answer for this lie.

THE BARBARIAN: What do you mean, you impudent man? I do not acknowledge any God.

THE DYING MAN: Forgive me, brother; I fear that you know nothing about Him. He whom I adore is renewing my strength in order to tell you, with the voice of a dying man, that if you believe in God you should treat me charitably. He gave me my wife and children; do not make them die in misery. As regards my body, you may do what you wish with it; I surrender it entirely to you. But believe in God, I implore you.

THE BARBARIAN: You must do as I have said without any further reasoning. That is what I want, I command you.

THE DYING MAN: And why are you interested in tormenting me?

THE BARBARIAN: What? Why am I interested? If I had your signature, I would then get a good office in the Church.

THE DYING MAN: Ah! My brother! My last few moments have arrived. I am about to die. I shall ask God to touch your heart and convert you.

THE BARBARIAN: To hell with that impertinent man who failed to sign. I shall forge his signature and sign for him.

The following letter confirms the same kind of moral thinking.

SEVENTEEN

A Letter written to the Jesuit Le Tellier,[1] by a Beneficed Correspondent, 6 May 1714[*]

Reverend Father,

I obey the orders that your reverence gave me to provide the most appropriate means to deliver Jesus and his Society from their enemies. I believe that there are no more than 500,000 Huguenots in the kingdom, although some people estimate 1,000,000, and others 1,500,000. But no matter how many there are, here is my advice, which I submit very humbly to your judgement, as I ought.

1. It is easy to arrest in a single day all the preachers and to hang them all in the same place, not only to edify the public, but also because it would be a beautiful spectacle.

2. I would have all mothers and fathers assassinated in their beds, because it might provoke a riot if they were killed in the streets. Besides, some of them might succeed in escaping, which is something that should be avoided above all else. Such an execution follows necessarily from our principles: for, if we are obliged to kill an individual heretic, as so many great theologians conclude, then it follows that all heretics must be killed.[2]

---

[*] When this was written in 1762 the Jesuits had not been abolished in France. If they had suffered misfortune, the author would certainly have respected them. But let people remember for ever that they were persecuted only because they themselves were persecutors, so that their example may frighten those who are even more intolerant and who would hope some day to oppress fellow citizens who do not share their harsh and absurd views.

3. I would arrange the following day to marry all the girls to good Catholics, since it is not necessary to depopulate the State too much after the most recent war.[3] But as regards boys who are fourteen or fifteen years old and are already imbued with false principles that one could not hope to eradicate, my view is that they must all be castrated, so that this breed may never be reproduced. As regards other young boys, they should be educated in our colleges and should be flogged until they know by heart the works of Sanchez and Molina.[4]

4. I think, subject to correction, that one should apply the same measures to all the Lutherans in Alsace, because in 1704 I saw two old ladies from that region laughing on the day we were defeated in the Battle of Höchstädt.[5]

5. The case of Jansenists will perhaps appear more awkward. I believe there are at least six million of them, but someone with a mind like yours should not be afraid of that. I include with the Jansenists all the *parlements* that so outrageously uphold the freedoms of the Gallican Church. It is up to your reverence to evaluate, with your customary prudence, the means by which all these cantankerous spirits can be forced to submit to you. The Gunpowder Plot failed to achieve its objective because one of the conspirators was indiscreet enough to try to save the life of one of his friends. But, since you have no friends, there is no danger of a similar unfortunate outcome. It would be very easy for you to blow up all the *parlements* of the kingdom by using the discovery of the monk Schwartz, which is called *pulvis pyrius*.[6] I calculate that you would need thirty-six barrels of gunpowder for each *parlement*, and thus by multiplying twelve *parlements* by thirty-six barrels, that would amount to only 432 barrels, which – at a hundred écus per barrel – adds up to a total of 129,600 pounds. That is a mere pittance for the reverend Father General. Once the *parlements* are blown up, you may transfer their offices to members

of your Society, who are perfectly familiar with the laws
of the kingdom.

6. It will be easy to poison Cardinal de Noailles,[7] who is a
simple man and is not suspicious of anything.

Your reverence will use similar methods to convert
some uncooperative bishops. Their dioceses will be
transferred to Jesuits by a papal decision. When all the
bishops have agreed to support our cause and all the
curates are appointed by the bishops, this is what I
would advise, subject to agreement by your reverence.

7. Since the Jansenists are said to receive Communion at
least at Easter, it would not be a bad idea to sprinkle the
hosts with the drug that was used to bring the emperor
Henry VII[8] to justice. Some critic might possibly object
that this operation would risk poisoning the Molinists
as well.[9] That is a serious objection. But there are no
plans without some drawbacks and there is no system
that does not threaten ruin in some place or other. If
one were put off by such minor difficulties, one would
never do anything. Besides, since this is a question of
achieving the greatest possible good, one should not be
scandalized if this great good has some unpalatable
consequences that are completely trivial.

We have no reason to reproach ourselves. It is evident that all
the so-called reformers and all the Jansenists are destined for
Hell. Thus all we are doing is hastening the day when they get
there.

It is equally clear that Paradise belongs by right to the
Molinists. Therefore, if we cause their death inadvertently and
without any evil intention, we accelerate their heavenly joy.[10]
We are the servants of Providence in both cases.

As regards those who may be alarmed slightly by the numbers involved, your reverence could remind them that, from
the early days of the Church up to 1707[11] – that is, for approximately fourteen centuries – theology has procured the massacre
of more than fifty million people, whereas I propose to

strangle, poison or cut the throat of only about six and a half million more.

There might be a further objection that my estimate of the numbers involved is inaccurate and that I have miscalculated in some way. For, it might be said, if in fourteen centuries only fifty million people have perished because of theological distinctions, dilemmas and counter-arguments, that amounts to an annual total of only 35,714 people (plus a fraction of a person) and that therefore I would kill an extra 6,464,285 people (and a fraction) in this year alone. But this quibbling is truthfully very childish; one could even say that it is impious. For is it not obvious that I save the lives of all Catholics until the end of time? One would never be finished if one had to reply to all such critics. I remain, with the greatest respect, reverend Father,

The very humble, very devout, and very compassionate R.

A native of Angoulême,[12] Prefect of the Congregation.

It was impossible to implement this plan because Father Le Tellier had some objections to it and his reverence was exiled the following year.[13] But since one ought to consider the pros and cons of any plan, it is good to consider if there are some situations in which one could legitimately adopt the advice of Father Le Tellier's correspondent. It seems as if it might be harsh to implement all the details of this proposal. But one must consider the circumstances in which different remedies should be applied – to torture, hang or send to the galleys those people who do not share our views. That is the issue that I address in the next chapter.

EIGHTEEN

The Only Circumstances in which Intolerance is Legally Justified

If a government is not to have a right to punish human errors, those errors must not be crimes. They are crimes only when they are detrimental to society, and they damage society as soon as they inspire fanaticism. Therefore, in order to deserve toleration, people must begin by avoiding fanaticism.

If a few young Jesuits knew that the Church disapproved of them, that the Jansenists were condemned by a papal bull (and are therefore also disapproved of) and if they began to set fire to a house belonging to the priests of the Oratory[1] because Quesnel[2] was a Jansenist, it is clear that it would be necessary to punish those Jesuits.

Likewise, if they preached criminal advice or if their institution were in breach of the laws of the kingdom, there would be no objection to dissolving their congregation and abolishing the Jesuits in order to turn them into good citizens. To abolish them would be ultimately a purely imaginary evil and a real benefit to them, for what could be wrong with wearing a short coat instead of a cassock or being free rather than a slave? Whole regiments are demobilized in peacetime and no one objects to that; why do the Jesuits complain so loudly when they are reformed for the sake of peace in the Church?[3]

If the Franciscans were motivated by religious zeal in favour of the Virgin Mary and went to demolish a church that belonged to the Dominicans because they believed that Mary was born in original sin, one would then have to treat the Franciscans more or less like the Jesuits.

One would say the same thing about the Lutherans and Calvinists. They might well say: 'We follow the guidance of our conscience and it is better to obey God rather than men.[4] We are the genuine Christian flock and we should exterminate the wolves.' It is evident, however, that they are wolves themselves.

One of the most remarkable examples of fanaticism was a small sect in Denmark, whose guiding principle was the best in the world. Those people wished to gain eternal life for their fellow citizens, but the consequences of their principle were very peculiar. They knew that all young children who die before they are baptized are damned, and that those who are lucky enough to die immediately after being baptized enjoy eternal happiness in Heaven. They therefore set out to cut the throat of every newly baptized boy or girl that they could find. Without doubt they thereby conferred on them the greatest possible benefit. At one and the same time, they protected them from original sin, from the miseries of this life and from eternal Hell, and sent them infallibly to Heaven.[5] But people like that did not appreciate that it is not permissible to do some small evil deed in order to gain a great good, that they had no right over the lives of these children, and that most fathers and mothers are sufficiently carnal to prefer having the company of their boys and girls rather than seeing their throats cut to get into Paradise. In brief, magistrates should punish homicide, even if it is committed with good intentions.

The Jews seem to have more right than anyone else to dispossess and murder us. For although there are numerous examples of toleration in the Old Testament, there are also some severe actions and severe laws there. God commanded them occasionally to kill idolaters and to spare only marriageable girls. They regard us as idolaters and, although we tolerate them today, they could easily kill us off and spare only our marriageable daughters if they had the power to do so.

They would be especially under an indispensable obligation to assassinate all the Turks. That would be taken for granted, because the Turks occupy the land of the Hethites, Jebusites, Amorrhites, Gergesites, Hevites, Aracites, Sinites, Hamathites and Samarites, all of whom were subject to a curse.[6] Their land, which was more than twenty-five leagues long, was given to the Jews by several consecutive treaties. They ought to return to their own lands, where Muslims have been usurpers for more than a thousand years.

If Jews were to reason along those lines today, it is clear that the only response one could make to them would be to impale them.

These are more or less the only circumstances in which intolerance seems to be reasonable.

NINETEEN

An Account of a Controversial Disagreement in China

During the early years of the reign of the emperor Kangxi, a mandarin in the town of Canton heard a great noise coming from the house next door and he asked if someone had been killed. He was told that a chaplain from a Danish congregation, a Dutch chaplain and a Jesuit were engaged in a dispute. He invited them in to visit his house, gave them tea and preserves, and asked them what they were quarrelling about.

The Jesuit told him that, since he was always right, he found it very difficult having to deal with people who were always wrong about things; he said that he had begun the discussion with the greatest restraint, but had eventually lost his patience.

The mandarin explained to them with the greatest discretion that good manners were necessary in any disagreement, that in China no one ever got angry, and he asked them what they were disputing about.

The Jesuit replied: 'My lord, I shall appoint you to be the judge. These two gentlemen refuse to submit to the decisions of the Council of Trent.'

'That surprises me,' said the mandarin and, turning towards the two stubborn gentlemen, he said: 'It seems to me, gentlemen, that you should respect the decisions of a large assembly. I do not know what the Council of Trent is. But several people are always better informed than one person alone. No one should believe that he knows more about some issue than others or that reason resides only in his own head. That is what our great Confucius[1] teaches. And if you accept what I say, you will do very well to accept what the Council of Trent teaches.'

The Danish chaplain then intervened and said: 'My lord speaks with the greatest wisdom. We respect large assemblies, just as we should do. But we are also entirely in agreement with several assemblies that were held before that of Trent.'

'Oh, if that is the case,' said the mandarin, 'I beg your pardon and you may well be right. On that score you are of the same opinion – the Dutchman and yourself – in opposition to this unfortunate Jesuit.'

'Not at all,' said the Dutchman. 'This man here holds views that are as extraordinary as those of the Jesuit, who was being disingenuous with you. There is no way I could agree with him.'

'I do not understand you,' said the mandarin. 'Is it not the case that all three of you are Christians? Do all three of you not come to teach Christianity in our empire? And should you not, therefore, hold the same doctrines?'

'You see, my lord,' said the Jesuit, 'these two men here are mortal enemies and both of them disagree with me. It is therefore obvious that both of them are wrong and that reason supports only my view.'

'That is not obvious,' said the mandarin. 'It would be entirely possible that all three of you are wrong. I would be interested to hear each one of you in turn.'

The Jesuit then delivered a long speech, in the course of which the Dane and the Dutchman shrugged their shoulders and the mandarin did not understand a word of what he said. The Dane then took his turn to speak, while his two opponents looked on him with pity and the mandarin understood no more than in the first speech. The Dutchman was just as unsuccessful. Finally, all three of them spoke at the same time and hurled insults at each other. The polite mandarin had great difficulty in putting a stop to them, and said: 'If you wish your teaching to be tolerated here, you should begin by not being intolerant or intolerable.'

As they were leaving the meeting, the Jesuit met a Dominican missionary. He told him that he had won the argument and assured him that truth always prevails. The Dominican told him: 'If I had been there, you would not have won the argument. I would have convicted you of lies and idolatry.' The discussion then became heated and the Jesuit and Dominican grabbed each other by the hair. The mandarin, when he found out about their scandalous conduct, sent them both to prison. A deputy mandarin said to the judge: 'How long does Your Excellency wish to keep them behind bars?' 'Until they come to some agreement between them,' said the judge. 'Ah!' said the deputy mandarin, 'in that case they will be in prison for the rest of their lives.' 'Well, then,' said the judge, 'until they forgive each other.' 'They will never forgive each other,' said the deputy, 'I know what they are like.' 'Well, then,' said the judge, 'they must remain in prison until they pretend to forgive each other.'

TWENTY

Is it Useful to Keep People in their Superstitions?

The weakness and perversity of the human race are such that it is undoubtedly much better for people to be under the influence of every possible superstition than to live without religion, on condition that the superstitions do not incite people to murder. Human beings have always needed some kind of restraint, and although it was ridiculous to offer sacrifices to fauns, elves or nymphs, it was much more reasonable and more useful to adore such fantastic images of the Divinity than to surrender to atheism. A rational, violent and powerful atheist would be as fatal a scourge as a bloodthirsty superstitious person.[1]

When people have no sensible concepts of the Divinity, false notions take their place, just as counterfeit money is used during hard times when authentic money is in short supply. A pagan was restrained from committing crime by fear of being punished by false gods; a Malabar feared being punished by his pagoda. Wherever a society is established, some religion is necessary. The laws oversee known crimes, while religion controls secret crimes.

But once people come to embrace a pure and holy religion, superstition becomes not only useless but very dangerous. One should not try to nourish with acorns those whom God deigns to nourish with bread.

Superstition is related to religion as astrology is to astronomy, i.e., as the very foolish daughter of a very wise mother. These two daughters have held the whole world in subjection for a long time.

During the centuries of barbarism, when one could hardly find two feudal lords who possessed a copy of the New Testament, it may have been excusable to present fables to the common people, including the feudal lords, their imbecile wives and their vulgar vassals. They had them believe that St Christopher carried the infant Jesus from one bank of a river to the other; they were fed on stories of witchcraft and demonic possession; they easily imagined that St Genou cured people of gout and that St Clare healed diseased eyes.[2] Children believed in the werewolf and their fathers believed in St Francis's cincture of rope. There were innumerable relics in use.

The remnants of many superstitions survived for some time among people even when religion had eventually been purified. It is well known that when M. de Noailles, the bishop of Châlons, had an alleged relic of Christ's sacred navel removed and thrown into the fire, the whole town of Châlons initiated proceedings against him.[3] But his courage matched his piety and he eventually succeeded in persuading the people of Champagne that it is possible to adore Jesus Christ in spirit and in truth without having his navel in the church.

Those who were called Jansenists contributed significantly to uprooting gradually from the spirit of the nation many false ideas that discredited the Christian religion. People ceased to believe that praying to the Virgin Mary for thirty days would be enough to obtain anything they wished or to make them free to sin with impunity.

The common people eventually began to suspect that it was not St Genevieve who caused or prevented the rain, but it was God Himself who controlled the elements. Monks were surprised that their saints no longer performed miracles; and if the authors of the *Life of St Francis Xavier* were to return to earth today they would not dare claim that this saint brought nine dead people back to life again, that he bilocated on land and sea, and that when his crucifix fell into the sea a crayfish returned it to him.[4]

The same applies to excommunications. Our historians tell us that when Pope Gregory V excommunicated King Robert because he married his godmother Princess Bertha his servants threw the food they had prepared for the king out of the window and that as punishment for her incest Queen Bertha gave birth to a goose.[5] It is doubtful if cooks who worked for an excommunicated king of France today would throw his dinner out of the window or that the queen would give birth to a gosling in a similar situation.

If there are any convulsionaries in a corner of the Paris suburbs, they must have an illness that comes from lice and affects only the most unclean members of the population.[6] Day by day reason penetrates France and reaches into merchants' shops as much as the great houses of the nobility. We must therefore cultivate the fruits of this rationality, especially since it is impossible to prevent them from blossoming. Now that France has been enlightened by people such as Pascal, Nicole, Arnauld, Bossuet, Descartes, Gassendi, Bayle, Fontenelle[7] and others, it is impossible to govern it in the same way as it was governed in the time of Garasse and Menot.[8]

If those who teach errors – by which I mean those great teachers who were paid and honoured for such a long time to brutalize the human race – were to command people to believe that a seed must rot in order to germinate;[9] that the Earth is immobile on its foundations and that it does not revolve around the Sun; that the tides are not a natural effect of gravitation or that the rainbow does not result from the refraction and reflection of rays of light, etc., and if they relied on poorly understood passages of Holy Scripture to support their commands, how would educated people regard them? Would the term 'stupid'[10] be too strong? And if these wise teachers used force and persecution to impose their insolent ignorance on others, would the description 'wild animals' be inappropriate?

The more we despise the superstitions of monks, the more we respect bishops and value their curates. The latter do only what is good, while monastic superstitions from across the Alps[11] would do much harm. But is it not the case that the most dangerous of all superstitions is that we should hate our neighbours because of what they believe? And is it not obvious that it would be much more reasonable to worship the holy navel, the holy foreskin, the milk and the robe of the Virgin Mary, than for us to detest and persecute other human beings?

TWENTY-ONE

Virtue is Better than Knowledge

The fewer dogmas there are, the fewer disputes about them, and the fewer disputes, the less harm done. If that is not true, then I am mistaken.

Religion was established in order to make us happy in this life and in the life to come. What is required in order to be happy in the next life? One has to be just.

What is required in order to be happy in this life, insofar as the misery of our nature allows? One must be tolerant.

It would be the height of folly for someone to claim to have persuaded all human beings to agree about everything in metaphysics. It would be much easier to conquer the whole world by force of arms than to subjugate all the human minds in a single town.

In contrast, Euclid easily succeeded in convincing all human beings of the truths of geometry. Why? Because every one of them is an evident conclusion from this little axiom: *Two and two are four*. It is not quite the same when metaphysics and theology are combined.

When Bishop Alexander and the priest Arios or Arius began to dispute about how the Word emanated from the Father, the emperor Constantine first wrote to them as follows (which is reported by Eusebius and Socrates): 'You are very foolish to argue about things that you cannot possibly understand.'[1]

If the two disputing parties had been wise enough to recognize that the Emperor was right, the Christian world would have avoided three hundred years of bloodshed.

Indeed, what could be more foolish and abhorrent than to say to people: 'My friends, it is not enough to be faithful subjects, submissive children, sensitive fathers and honest neighbours; it is not sufficient to practise all the virtues, to cultivate friendships, to flee from ingratitude and to adore Jesus Christ peacefully. You must also know how he was begotten from all eternity. And if you do not know how to distinguish between the *homoousion* in the hypostasis, we declare that you will be burned in Hell for ever and, meantime, we shall begin by cutting your throats.'[2]

If such a decision had been presented to someone like Archimedes or Posidonius or Varro or Cato or Cicero, what would they have replied?[3]

Constantine did not implement his decision to impose silence on the two disputants. He could have summoned those paradigms of sophistry to his palace and asked them by what authority they disturbed the peace of the world: 'Are you certain about the titles of the divine family? What does it matter to you if the Word was "made" or "begotten" as long as people are faithful to God, that a good moral doctrine is preached and that it is practised as much as possible? I have committed many sins in my life and so have you. You are ambitious, as I am; governing the Empire has involved me in some deceit and cruelty and I have assassinated almost everyone who was close to me. I repent of all that. I wish to expiate my crimes by bringing peace to the Roman Empire. Do not prevent me from the one good thing that could erase the memory of my past barbarities. Help me to finish my days in peace.' He may not have persuaded the two disputing parties with this speech. He may have been flattered to preside at a Church council in a long red robe, with his head crowned with gems.[4]

That, however, is what opened the door to all the scourges that originated in Asia and then inundated the West. Every disputed scriptural text gave rise to a furious row, in which the disputing parties were armed with a sophism in one hand and a dagger in the other, and which made everyone involved cruel and irrational. The Huns, the Heruli, the Goths and the Vandals who came later caused infinitely less damage and the worst thing they did was to become involved in these fatal disputes.

TWENTY-TWO

Universal Tolerance

It does not require great skill or rare eloquence to prove that Christians should tolerate each other. I would even go further and say that we should think of all human beings as our brothers. What? A Turk as a brother? A Chinaman as a brother? Jews and people from Siam as brothers too? Yes, without doubt, for are we not all children of the same Father and creatures of the same God?

But someone might object: these people despise us, they treat us as idolaters! Well! I would tell them that they are very much mistaken. It seems to me that I could at least surprise the proud stubbornness of an imam or of a Buddhist monk if I spoke to them more or less as follows:

This little globe, which is merely a dot, revolves in space just like so many other globes, in the vast extent of which we are all lost. A human being, who is about five feet high, is certainly a negligible entity in this creation. One of those imperceptible beings says to some of their neighbours, in Arabia or in South Africa: 'Listen to me, because the God of all the worlds has enlightened me; there are 900 million little ants like us on Earth, but there is only one anthill that is cherished by God. He has hated all the others since the beginning of time. My anthill will therefore be the only happy one and all the others will be eternally miserable.'

They would surely stop me and ask what fool speaks like that. I would have to reply to them: 'It is yourselves who say these things.' I would then try to calm them, but it would be rather difficult.

I would then speak to Christians and I would venture to say, for example, to a Dominican judge who serves in the

Inquisition: 'My brother, you know that every region in Italy has its own dialect and that they do not speak in Venice or Bergamo in the same way as they do in Florence. The Academy of Crusca[1] has standardized the language; its dictionary provides the rules that people must observe and the grammar of Buonmattei[2] is an infallible guide that they must follow. But do you think that the head of the Academy or, in his absence, Buonmattei could have been morally justified in cutting out the tongues of all the Venetians or the natives of Bergamo who continued to speak their own dialect?'

The inquisitor replies to me: 'There is a big difference between the two cases. I am concerned with the salvation of your soul. It is for your own good that the Director of the Inquisition commands that you be arrested on the sworn statement of a single witness, even if he or she is infamous and an ex-convict; that you have no access to a lawyer to defend you; that even the name of your accuser be withheld from you; that the inquisitor promises to be favourable to you and then condemns you; that he makes you suffer five different kinds of torture and that you are then whipped or sent to hard labour or ceremoniously burned.* Father Ivonet, Dr Cucalón, Zachinos, Campeggi, Rojas, Felynus, Gambarus, Diabarus, Gambellinus,[3] are explicit about this and it is impossible to disagree with them.'

I would take the liberty of replying to him: 'My dear brother, you may possibly be right; I am convinced that you are trying to be good to me; but could I not be saved without all that?'

It is true that these absurd horrors do not soil the face of the Earth every day. But they have occurred frequently, and one could easily compose a book about them that is much larger than the Gospels and would be enough to condemn them. Not

---

* See the excellent book entitled *The Manual of the Inquisition*. [*Ed.* A book discovered and published by André Morellet (1727–1819), entitled: *Le Manuel des inquisiteurs à l'usage d'Espagne et de Portugal, ou abrégé de l'ouvrage intitulé: 'Directorium Inquisitorum' composé vers 1358 par Nicolas Eymeric* {The Manual of Inquisitors for use in Spain and Portugal, or an abridgement of the work entitled: A Directory for Inquisitors, composed about 1358 by Nicolas Eymerich} (Lisbon, 1762).]

only is it very cruel, in this short life, to persecute those who do not think as we do, but it seems as if it is rather risky to pronounce their eternal damnation. It seems to me that it hardly belongs to evanescent atoms, as we are, to anticipate in that way the decisions of the Creator. I do not disagree at all with the following axiom: 'Outside the Church there is no salvation.'[4] I respect that teaching, just as I respect everything that the Church teaches. But, truthfully, do we really know all the ways of God and the full scope of His compassion? Are we not allowed to hope in Him as much as we fear Him? Is it not enough to be faithful to the Church? Must each individual usurp the rights of the Divinity and decide in His place the eternal fate of all human beings?

When we mourn the death of a king of Sweden, Denmark, England or Prussia do we think we are in mourning for a condemned man who will burn in Hell eternally? There are forty million people in Europe who are not members of the Church of Rome and should we say to each of them: 'Sir, given the fact that you are infallibly damned, I do not wish to dine in your company, to speak to you or to have anything to do with you'?

What French ambassador, when presenting his credentials to the Sultan of Turkey, would say to himself secretly: Your Highness will infallibly burn for all eternity, because you were circumcised? If he genuinely believed that the Sultan was God's mortal enemy and the object of divine vengeance, could he even talk to him? Should he have been sent to him as an ambassador? If someone were truly convinced of the idea that they were dealing with those who are condemned, how could they engage in normal business with them or ever extend to them the duties of civil life?

O followers of a compassionate God: if you were cruel in your hearts; if while adoring Him whose entire law consisted in the following words, 'Love God and your neighbour',[5] you have buried this pure and holy law under a heap of sophisms and incomprehensible disputes; if you have stirred up discord, sometimes for the sake of a new word or even one letter of the alphabet;[6] if you have linked eternal punishments with the mere omission of a few words or a few ceremonies that some people could not have known about,[7] I would say to you, as I weep for the whole human race: 'Come with me to the day when all human beings will be judged, when God will judge everyone according to their works.

'I see all the dead of previous centuries and of our own era being summoned before Him. Are you certain that our Creator and our Father will say to the wise and virtuous Confucius, to Solon the lawgiver, to Pythagoras, to Zaleucus, Socrates and Plato, to the divine Antoninus, to the good Trajan, to Titus, who were adornments of the human race, to Epictetus and so many others who were model human beings:[8] Be off, monsters! Go and suffer infinitely long and intense punishments and may your sufferings be as eternal as I am! And you, my beloved Jean Châtel, Ravaillac, Damiens, Cartouche[9] and others who died with the last rites, come share at my right side with me in my empire and happiness.'

Do you recoil in horror at these words? Now that I have uttered them, I have nothing further to say to you.

TWENTY-THREE

A Prayer to God

I no longer address other people, but I address You, the God of all beings, all worlds and all ages. If feeble creatures – who are imperceptible to the rest of the universe and lost in its immensity – are allowed to dare request something from You who have given everything and whose decrees are immutable and eternal: deign to look with pity on the mistakes that result from our nature, lest they lead to disaster. You did not give us a heart so that we could hate each other or hands to kill each other. Grant that we may help each other to bear the burden of a short and painful life; that the slight differences in the clothes that cover our fragile bodies, the differences between our inadequate languages, variations in all our ridiculous customs, imperfect laws and foolish opinions, differences between all the social conditions that are so important to us and so trivial to You; that all the little nuances that distinguish the atoms known as human beings may not become occasions for hatred and persecution! Grant that those who light candles during daylight to honour You may tolerate those who are content with the light of the Sun; that those who cover their clothes with white linen as a sign that they love You may not detest those who express the same sentiment by wearing a coat of black wool; that it be equally appropriate to adore You in a dialect that derives from some ancient language or in a more recent dialect; that those whose clothes are died in red or purple and who are lords over a small patch of a small heap of the mud of this Earth, and who possess some circular fragments of a certain metal, may enjoy without pride what they call 'grandeur' and 'riches', and that others may observe them without being envious; for You know that there is nothing worth envying and no justification for any pride in these vanities.

May all human beings remember that they are brothers. May they be horrified as much by the tyranny that is exercised over souls as when they condemn robberies that forcefully steal the fruits of honest toil and peaceful work. If the scourges of war are unavoidable, let us at least not hate each other and tear each other apart in peacetime, and let us use the short period of our existence to bless Your bounty, which has granted us this moment, in a thousand different and equally good languages from Siam to California.

TWENTY-FOUR

Postscript

While I was writing this work with the sole objective of making people more compassionate and charitable, someone else wrote a book with exactly the opposite intention, for everyone has their own opinion. This author published a short guide for persecuting people, entitled *The Harmony of Religion and Humanity*[1] (which must surely be a printer's error; it should read instead *Inhumanity*).

The author of this pious libel relies on St Augustine, who, having initially preached toleration, eventually preached in favour of persecution, since he had then become more powerful and he often changed his mind. He also quotes Bossuet, the Bishop of Meaux, who persecuted the celebrated Fénelon, Archbishop of Cambrai, for having published the suggestion that it is worth loving God for His own sake.

I accept that Bossuet was eloquent. I also accept that the Bishop of Hippo,[2] although he was often inconsistent, was more eloquent than other Africans. But I take the liberty of saying, with Armande, in Molière's *The Learned Women*:

> If one wishes to be guided by someone,
> One should imitate them in their virtues.[3]

I would say to the Bishop of Hippo: Monsignor, you have changed your mind, but allow me to adopt your previous opinion, because, in truth, I think it was better.

I would say to the Bishop of Meaux: you are a famous man and I find you at least as learned as St Augustine and much more eloquent. But why do you torment your fellow bishop so much, when he was just as eloquent as you in a different way and much more likeable?

The author of the pious libel about inhumanity is neither a Bossuet nor an Augustine. I think he would make an excellent Inquisitor; I wish he had been in Goa at the head of that wonderful tribunal. He is also a statesman and he lays out ambitious political principles. 'If there are many unorthodox believers among you,' he says, 'handle them carefully and persuade them. If there are only a few of them, then revert to the gallows and hard labour, and you will find those remedies very effective.' That is what he suggests[4] on pages 89 and 90.

Thank God I am a good Catholic and I have no fear of becoming what Huguenots call a 'martyr'. But if this author were ever to become Prime Minister – since he flatters himself in his holy libel that he might do so – I hereby inform him that I shall leave for England the very day he gets his seal of office.

In the mean time I can only thank Providence for making sure that people like him always argue very poorly. He goes so far as to quote Bayle among the supporters of intolerance.[5] That is very clever and appropriate; and from the fact that Bayle agrees that seditious and mischievous people should be punished our man concluded that we ought to persecute with fire and sword people of good faith who live peacefully.

Almost his whole book is a repetition of the *Defence of the St Bartholomew's Day Massacre*.[6] He is just like the previous apologist or his echo. In the case of either of them it is hoped that neither the master nor his pupil will ever govern the State.

But if it ever happens that they get into power, I make this request a long time in advance in relation to two lines from page 93 of the same pious libel: 'Is it necessary to sacrifice the welfare of the whole nation for the sake of one twentieth of the nation?'

If we assume that there are twenty Roman Catholics in France for every Huguenot, I would not imagine that the one Huguenot would devour the twenty Catholics. But likewise, why would the twenty Catholics devour the one Huguenot and why would they prevent this Huguenot from getting married? Are there not bishops, priests and monks who own lands in

Dauphiny, Gévaudan, Agde and Carcassonne?[7] Do these bishops, priests and monks not have some farm workers who unfortunately do not believe in transubstantiation? Are these bishops, priests, monks and the general public not concerned that these farm workers may have large families? And should those who receive communion only under one species be the only people who are allowed to have children?[8] In truth, that is neither just nor honest.

'The revocation of the Edict of Nantes has not caused as many disadvantages as people claim,' says our author.[9]

If anyone attributes more disadvantages to the revocation than it actually caused, then they exaggerate, although exaggerating is a mistake that almost all historians make. But it is equally a mistake for all the polemicists who make nothing of the evils for which they are responsible. Let us not believe either the professors of the University of Paris or the preachers of Amsterdam.

Let us accept Count d'Avaux[10] as judge, who was ambassador to Holland from 1685 to 1688. He says on page 181, volume five, that one man offered to locate more than twenty million pounds that the persecuted Huguenots transferred out of France. Louis XIV replied to Mr d'Avaux: 'The information that I receive every day about an infinite number of conversions leaves me in no doubt any longer that the most stubborn will follow the example of the others.'

It is evident from this letter that Louis XIV was very confident about the scope of his own power. He was told every morning: 'Sire, you are the greatest king in the universe; the whole universe will glory in agreeing with whatever you say, once you have spoken.' Pellison, who had enriched himself in the office of first clerk of the Treasury and had spent three years in the Bastille as an accomplice of Fouquet;[11] Pellison, who had been a Calvinist and then became a deacon and received a benefice, who published both prayers for the Mass and poems to Iris, and had secured the post of bursar and religious converter; Pellison, I say, delivered every three months a long list of renunciations at seven or eight écus each, and had his king believe that he could convert all the Turks at the same price. They took turns in deceiving the king; how could he have resisted being seduced?

The same Mr d'Avaux, however, informed the king that some individual called Vincent employed more than 500 workers near Angoulême and that it would be harmful if he were to emigrate (Vol. 5, p. 194).

The same Mr d'Avaux speaks about two regiments that the Prince of Orange had already recruited from among exiled French officers; he speaks about sailors who deserted from three French ships to serve in those of the Prince of Orange. In addition to these two regiments, the Prince of Orange is also forming a company of refugee cadets who are commanded by two captains (p. 240). This ambassador also writes, on 9 May 1686, to Mr de Seignelay, 'that he cannot hide his suffering at seeing French manufacturers transferring to Holland, where they plan to remain permanently'.

I add to all these testimonies those of all the intendants of the kingdom in 1698, and you may then judge if the revocation of the Edict of Nantes has done more harm than good, despite the opinion of the respected author of *The Harmony of Religion and Humanity*.

A Marshal of France[12] who was known for his superior intelligence said some years ago: 'I do not know if dragonnades were necessary, but it is necessary now not to continue the practice any more.'

I agree that I initially thought I went a bit too far by publishing the letter of Father Le Tellier's correspondent, in which a member of a religious congregation proposed using barrels of gunpowder. I used to think that no one would believe me about that, and that people would think that the letter was forged. I was happily relieved of my scruples when I read the following compassionate words on page 149 of *The Harmony of Religion and Humanity*: 'The total extermination of Protestants in France will not weaken France any more than bloodletting a patient with a strong constitution.'

This compassionate Christian, who had just said that Protestants constitute one twentieth of the nation, wishes therefore to spill the blood of this twentieth fraction and thinks of this operation as nothing more significant than using a palette in a phlebotomy. May God protect us together with him from the three twentieths![13]

If, therefore, a respectable gentleman proposes to kill one twentieth of the nation, why could the friend of Father Le Tellier not have proposed to blow up, kill and poison a third of them? It is, therefore, very likely that the letter to Father Le Tellier is genuine.

The pious author eventually finishes by concluding that intolerance is an excellent thing 'because,' he says, 'it was not explicitly condemned by Jesus Christ'. But Jesus Christ did not condemn those who would set fire to the whole of Paris either. Would that be a reason to canonize such arsonists?

Thus, whenever the gentle and beneficent voice of Nature is heard speaking from one direction, fanaticism – that great enemy of Nature – howls in protest. And whenever human beings are close to enjoying peace, intolerance goes to war against it. You who are the arbiters among nations, who have delivered peace to Europe, let you decide between the spirit of peace and the spirit of murder.

TWENTY-FIVE

Sequel and Conclusion

We know that the entire Council of State assembled at Versailles on 7 March 1763, that the government ministers attended and that the Chancellor[1] presided. Mr de Crosne,[2] the Master of Requests, reported on the Calas affair to the Council with the impartiality of a judge, the precision of someone who was fully informed and the simple and truthful eloquence of an orator and statesman, which was uniquely appropriate for such an assembly. A huge crowd of people of various social ranks waited in the gallery of the palace to hear the decision. The king was informed, within a short time, that the whole Council had decided unanimously that the Toulouse *parlement* must submit to the Council all the documentation related to the Calas trial, together with the reasons for the verdict that caused Jean Calas to die on the wheel. His Majesty approved the Council's decision.

There is, therefore, some justice and humanity among human beings, especially in the Council of a king who is deservedly loved. The affair concerning an unfortunate family of obscure citizens attracted the attention of His Majesty, his ministers, the Chancellor and the entire Council, and it was discussed with the same degree of critical scrutiny that the most important questions of war and peace would warrant. A love of justice and the interests of the human race guided all the judges. Thanks be to the God of mercy, who alone inspires justice and all the virtues!

We hereby confirm that we have never met the unfortunate Calas, whom the eight judges at Toulouse executed on the most unreliable evidence, in breach of the commands of our kings and the laws of all nations. Nor did we meet his son

Marc-Antoine, whose strange death prompted those judges to make their mistake, nor the mother, who is as respectable as she is unhappy, nor her innocent daughters, who travelled with her 200 leagues to present their disastrous experience and their virtue at the feet of the king.

God knows that we were motivated only by the spirit of justice, truth and peace when we published our views about toleration after the spirit of intolerance caused the death of Jean Calas.

We did not intend to offend the eight judges of Toulouse when we said that they were mistaken, which is what the entire Council also concluded. On the contrary, we provided them with an opportunity to clear their names before the whole of Europe. That would require acknowledging that inconclusive evidence and the demands of an irrational mob had overcome their sense of justice. It would include asking forgiveness of the widow and providing compensation as much as possible for the complete ruin of an innocent family by supporting those who now help its members in their distress. The judges caused the death of the father unjustly; it is now up to them to assume the responsibilities of a father for his children, on condition that these orphans are willing to accept such a feeble sign of a most just repentance. It will be good for the judges to make the offer, and for the family to decline the offer.

It is especially up to Mr David, the chief magistrate at Toulouse, to provide an example of his remorse since he was the first to persecute an innocent man. He insulted a father of a family who was dying on the scaffold. That level of cruelty is really unprecedented. But since God forgives, human beings should also forgive those who atone for their injustices.

The following letter was written from Languedoc on 20 February 1763:

Your book about toleration seems to me to be full of humanity and truth. But I fear that it will do more harm than good to the Calas family. It may antagonize the eight judges who decided in favour of death on the wheel. They will request the *parlement* to have your book burned and the fanatics – of whom there are

always many about – will reply with expressions of anger against
the voice of Reason, etc.

Here is my reply:

The eight judges of Toulouse may have my book burned if
they wish, since nothing could be easier. The *Provincial Letters*,[3] which are without doubt much more significant, were
also burned. Anyone may burn in their own home whatever
books or papers they dislike.

My book cannot do any harm or good to the Calas family,
whom I do not know. The king's Council, which is firm and
impartial, judges according to the laws and is guided by equity,
the rules of procedure and the evidence presented to the court,
and not by some writing which has no juridical status and
which is not in any way relevant to what the Council has to
decide.

One could print tracts in favour of or against the eight
judges of Toulouse, and for or against toleration, but neither
the Council nor any other tribunal would consider such books
as relevant evidence for their decision.[4]

This writing about toleration is a request that humanity presents very humbly to those in power who exercise prudence. I
sow a seed that may in due course produce a harvest. Let us
wait as long as is necessary for the king's bounty, the wisdom
of his ministers and the spirit of rationality that is beginning to
shed its light everywhere.

Nature says to all people: 'I have caused you all to be born
weak and ignorant, to live for a few brief moments on this
Earth before enriching it with your corpses. Since you are
weak, you should help each other; since you are ignorant, you
should enlighten and support each other. If it were ever the
case that you all agreed about some issue – which will never
happen – and if there were only one person who held a different view, you ought to forgive them, because I am the one who
is responsible for that dissident view. I gave you hands in order
to cultivate the earth and a small flicker of reason to guide you.
I placed a seed of compassion in your hearts so that you can
help each other to cope with life. Do not smother this seed, do

not corrupt it; you should realize that it is divine, and do not substitute pathetic scholastic disputes for the voice of Nature.

'I alone continue, despite your resistance, to unite you by your mutual needs in the very midst of the cruel wars that you wage for trivial reasons, in the eternal theatre of mistakes, bad luck and misfortune. I alone prevent the fatal consequences, within any nation, of the interminable divisions between the nobles and the judiciary, between those two bodies and the clergy, and between city-dwellers and farmers. They all ignore the limits of their rights, but, despite themselves, they all eventually listen to my voice, because it speaks to their hearts. I alone preserve justice in courts of law, where, without me, everything would be left to caprice and indecision in the midst of a confused pile of laws that were often enacted by chance or in response to some passing need, which differ from one province to another and from one town to another and are almost always inconsistent with other laws even in the same place. I alone can inspire justice, while laws inspire nothing other than bickering. Whoever listens to me will always judge well and those who merely try to reconcile inconsistent opinions will go astray.

'There is a very large edifice, the foundations of which I laid with my own hands.[5] It was solid and simple and everyone was able to enter it safely. People then decided to add to it the most bizarre, gross and useless ornaments, with the result that it is now falling apart on all sides, while people pick up the stones and hurl them at each other. I cry out to them: Stop! Remove these fatal bits of debris that are all your work and live with me in peace in the unshakeable edifice that is mine.'

An Additional Chapter: An Account of the Most Recent Decision in Favour of the Calas Family[1]

Two more years passed between the 7 March 1763 and the final judgement.[2] It is so easy for fanaticism to snatch life from innocent people and so difficult for Reason to deliver justice to them. It was impossible to avoid long delays, which inevitably resulted from various formalities. Insofar as these formalities had not been observed in the conviction of Calas, it was all the more important that the Council of State observe them to the letter. A full year was not enough to compel the Toulouse *parlement* to forward all the documents to Paris, to examine them and then report on them. This burdensome task was once again entrusted to Mr de Crosne. An assembly of almost eighty judges quashed the Toulouse verdict and ordered a complete retrial.

Almost all the tribunals of the kingdom were distracted with other important issues at that time. They pursued the Jesuits and abolished their order in France. The Jesuits had been intolerant and had persecuted others and they were now being persecuted themselves.

The farcical use of receipts for confession – a practice that the Jesuits were suspected of having initiated secretly and which they supported publicly – had already provoked the whole nation to hate them.[3] A major bankruptcy of one of their missionaries, which was believed to have resulted partly from fraud, was the last straw.[4] The mere association of the two words 'missionary' and 'bankrupt', which would seem to have nothing in common, was enough to persuade many people that they were guilty. Finally, the destruction of Port-Royal and the bones of so many famous people that were desecrated in their graves and exhumed at the beginning of the century, by orders that could have come only from the Jesuits, turned everyone against whatever little credibility they still retained. The history of their proscription can be read in the excellent book entitled *The Destruction of the Jesuits in France*, an impartial work – since it was written by a philosopher[5] – which is written with the exquisite style and eloquence of Pascal, and especially with a superior intelligence that is not compromised, as Pascal was, by prejudices that have often misled great minds.[6]

This great affair, in the course of which some supporters of the Jesuits claimed that religion itself had been abused, but in which most people thought it had been vindicated, distracted the public for several months and made them lose sight of the Calas trial. But since the king had assigned responsibility for the final judgement to the tribunal that is called the Court of Appeal, the same public that likes to flit from one scene to another forgot about the Jesuits and turned its attention once again to the Calas family.

The Court of Appeal is a sovereign court composed of Masters of Requests, which is responsible for deciding cases when different courts disagree and other cases that the king refers to it. It would be impossible to find a court that was better informed about the Calas affair. It included exactly the same magistrates who had twice made preliminary judgements about procedural issues in the appeal, and who were fully informed about the underlying issue and the way in which it had been decided in Toulouse. The widow of Jean Calas, his son and Mr Lavaisse all returned to prison. They brought all the way from Languedoc the elderly Catholic servant who had never left the side of her master and mistress during the evening when it was assumed, most improbably, that they were strangling their son and brother. The court considered exactly the same evidence that had been used to condemn Jean Calas to the wheel and to send his son into exile.

The eloquent Mr de Beaumont[7] made a new submission at that stage and another document was submitted by the young Mr Lavaisse, who had been so unjustly implicated in this criminal trial by the judges in Toulouse, who compounded their inconsistency by still failing to declare him innocent. This young man composed a submission that was universally considered worthy of comparison with that of Mr de Beaumont. He had the double advantage of speaking on his own behalf and on behalf of the family whose imprisonment he had shared. He could easily have gained his own release and walked free from the Toulouse prison if he had only agreed to say that he had momentarily left the mother and father alone during the time that they were supposed to have killed their son. They threatened to execute him; they offered him a choice between death and torture; a single word would have released him from jail. But he preferred to be exposed to torture than to utter that word, which would have been a lie. He revealed all these details in his candid submission that was so dignified, so simple and so completely lacking in all ostentation that he persuaded all those whom he wished merely to convince and, without wishing to become famous, he impressed everyone who heard him.

His father, who was a famous lawyer, had no part in composing his submission. He then found himself suddenly being compared with his son, who had never studied to become a lawyer.

Meanwhile very distinguished people flocked to the prison where Madame Calas and her daughters had been locked up together. They were moved to tears by the spectacle. Humanity and generosity helped the women enormously, while what is usually called 'charity' did nothing for them. Charity, which is so often petty and insulting, is characteristic of the so-called devout, and those people were still hostile to the Calas family.

The day came when innocence triumphed completely. Mr de Bacquencourt[8] had reported the whole trial and had studied the affair in the greatest possible detail; all the judges decided by a unanimous vote that the family was innocent and that they had been judged abusively and unjustly by the Toulouse *parlement*. They rehabilitated the memory of the father, Jean Calas. They allowed the family to appeal to the appropriate authorities to hold the judges accountable and to recover damages, costs and losses that the judges of Toulouse should have taken the initiative to offer.

There was universal joy in Paris. People gathered in public squares and streets. They came to see this family that had been so unhappy and were now so fully vindicated; they applauded as the judges passed by and heaped blessings on them. What made this spectacle all the more touching was that this day, the ninth of March, was the very same day that Calas had been most cruelly executed.

The Masters of Requests had delivered comprehensive justice to the Calas family and, by doing so, they had done nothing more than their duty. There is another duty, that of beneficence, with which courts comply less frequently, because they seem to think that they were established only to deliver justice. The Masters of Requests, however, decided to write collectively to ask His Majesty to compensate this family with gifts for the ruin they had suffered. That letter was duly written. The king responded by granting 36,000 pounds to the mother and her children; and of these 36,000 pounds, 3,000 pounds were included for the virtuous servant who had consistently defended the truth by supporting her employers.

By this act of bounty, as by so many other actions, the king earned the title that the nation's love had granted him.[9] May this example serve to inspire toleration among people, without which fanaticism would devastate the whole world or at least make it permanently miserable. We realize that this affair concerned only one family, while the anger of sects has been responsible for the deaths of thousands. But if the shadow of peace rests today over all Christian societies, following centuries of carnage, this tranquil time is the interval when the Calas tragedy should have the greatest impact, more or less as thunder does when it suddenly rumbles during the calm of a sunny day. Cases like this are rare, but they do occur, and they result from the depressing superstition that leads feeble minds to impute crimes to anyone who does not think as they do.

Notes

ONE

1. *Jean Calas ... sixty-eight*: In fact, he was sixty-four and Voltaire substituted his own age for that of Jean Calas. Voltaire used the age and fragile health of Calas as an argument in favour of his innocence.
2. *He was a Protestant ... modest allowance*: Jean Calas and his wife Anne-Rose Cabibel had four sons and two daughters. Louis, the third eldest, had converted to Catholicism and was no longer living at home, while Donat was working in Nîmes. Their two daughters Rosine and Nanette were also away from home on the evening of 13 October 1761.
3. *servant*: Jeanne Viguière.
4. *one of his friends*: Gaubert Lavaisse.
5. *Henri III ... Henry IV*: Henry III (1551–89) was assassinated by Jacques Clément in 1589 while laying siege to Paris in the course of the religious wars. Henry IV (1553–1610), who had been King of Navarre and a member of the Reformed Church, assumed the French crown as his successor and subsequently converted to Catholicism. He, too, was assassinated, in 1610, by François Ravaillac.
6. *massacre ... two centuries ago*: On 17 May 1562 a group of between three and five thousand Protestants took refuge in the town hall in Toulouse during a local outbreak of the religious wars that plagued France at the time. They agreed to lay down their arms in exchange for safe passage. Following their surrender, they were massacred by their Catholic opponents.
7. *obliged to assassinate ... Catholicism*: There was some basis for this view in Calvin's discussion of a child's duty to obey their parents, in *Institution de la religion chrestienne* {Institutes of the Christian Religion} (Book II, Chap. viii, sec. 36): 'The

Lord orders all who rebel against their parents to be put to death.'

8. *Mr David*: François-Raymond David de Beaudrigue, a municipal magistrate in Toulouse, was subsequently dismissed from office (12 February 1765) because of procedural irregularities in performing his official duties.

9. *A monitory*: A public demand (without naming any suspect, as apparently occurred in this case) by a bishop or vicar-general that anyone who had information about some event was obliged, on pain of excommunication from the Church, to reveal it to the relevant civil authorities.

10. *Duke of Fitz-James*: Charles, Duke of Fitz-James, became governor of Languedoc in 1761.

11. *His vote was decisive ... harsh judges*: A death sentence required a two-thirds majority. Thus, when the vote was provisionally seven to six (before one judge changed sides), the judge who ought to have recused himself provided the one-vote majority for conviction. The numbers reported by Voltaire do not add up, however, because the favourable judge mentioned in the text remained recused.

12. *a second verdict*: 18 March 1762.

13. *They locked him up ... Catholic faith*: Pierre Calas escaped from the priory on 4 July 1762 and travelled to Geneva, where Voltaire interviewed him.

14. *parlement*: The French regional *parlements* were not legislative bodies, but primarily judicial institutions that registered royal edicts for local implementation and applied them in their own regions. They also acted as courts of appeal against decisions taken by local magistrates. I retain the French spelling throughout to avoid confusion with modern legislative parliaments.

15. *the Pope is infallible ... cardinals*: The Catholic Church had believed for centuries that the truth of its doctrines concerning faith and morals was guaranteed by divine inspiration. As the magisterium of the Church became centralized in Rome, especially after the Council of Trent (1545–63), the indefectibility of the Church was transformed into the infallibility of the Pope when he taught in union with other bishops. The first Vatican Council (18 July 1870) taught 'as a divinely revealed dogma that when the Roman pontiff speaks ex cathedra [i.e.,] when he defines a doctrine concerning faith and morals to be held by the whole church, he possesses ... that infallibility which the divine Redeemer willed his church to enjoy in defining doctrine concerning faith and

morals', Norman P. Tanner, ed., *Decrees of the Ecumenical Councils* (London: Sheed & Ward, 1990), vol. II, p. 816.

16. *Father Houtteville*: Claude-François Houtteville (1686–1742) was the author of *La Religion Chrétienne, prouvée par les faits* {The Christian Religion, Proved by Facts} (1722), in the preface of which (1740 edn) he describes toleration as 'monstrous'.

TWO

1. *one of our ... wise magistrates*: Probably refers to Henri-François d'Aguesseau (1668–1751), who was appointed chancellor of France on three occasions and was described in similar complimentary terms in Voltaire's *Le Siècle de Louis XIV* {The Age of Louis XIV}. Voltaire alludes to the frequent reports of mystical experiences and religious visions in France in the seventeenth century, many of which were understood as the effects of demonic possession.

2. *The Brothers and Flagellants ... The League ... join a confraternity*: Voltaire refers to the religious wars in France in the sixteenth century; to the Catholic League that was founded by Henry I, Duke of Guise (1550–88), in 1576 to support the Catholic cause against Huguenots; and to various obscure medieval associations whose members practised extreme Christian rituals, such as flogging themselves in memory of the flogging of Christ.

THREE

1. *Pope Alexander VI*: (1492–1503) A nephew of Pope Callistus III (1455–58), he fathered five children.

2. *Julius II*: (1503–13) joined in the Holy League against France in 1511.

3. *Pope Leo X*: (1513–21).

4. *annates or reserved appointments*: Both terms refer to the role of the papacy in making appointments to senior ecclesiastical offices or benefices. The Holy See reserved the right to make all such appointments (e.g., to bishoprics) throughout the Catholic Church, and those who were appointed refunded the income from the first year of their benefice to Rome (which was called an 'annate').

5. *Mérindol and Cabrières*: Both located in the Vaucluse department in the south-east of France.

6.   *Waldensians*: Peter Waldo (fl. 1175) had initiated a reform movement in Lyon in 1173 and recommended that Christians return to the simple life of apostolic times. His followers were known as Waldensians and they subsequently became associated with the sixteenth-century reformers. In 1545 Francis I (1494–1547) provided troops who killed a large number of local Waldensian residents.

7.   *Dubourg*: Anne du Bourg (1521–59), who made public his conversion to Calvinism, was executed in December 1559.

8.   *massacre at Wassy*: When Francis, 2nd Duke of Guise (1519–63), was passing through Wassy in the Haute-Marne region in March 1562, he was informed that a group of Huguenots was holding a religious service in a local barn. When his efforts to prevent the service were foiled, his troops set fire to the barn and killed more than sixty Huguenots. This event is often identified as the start of the religious wars in France.

9.   *St Bartholomew's Day Massacre*: The most infamous massacre of Huguenots during the wars of religion. Catherine de' Medici (1519–89) was regent during the minority of her son Charles IX (reigned 1560–74). She authorized the massacre of Gaspard II de Coligny (1519–72) and his associates in Paris on 24 August 1572. The massacre continued for some weeks and spread throughout many French provinces, in the course of which it is estimated that 2,000 people were killed in Paris and at least 10,000 in the rest of France, although the exact numbers involved may have been higher.

10. *The Catholic League . . . the Feuillants*: See Chapter 1, note 5. François Ravaillac had spent a brief period as a member of the Feuillants, a reformed group of Cistercians who had been attached to the Abbey of Cîteaux and were granted independent status in 1586. They were abolished at the time of the French Revolution (1789) and their abbeys and schools were closed.

FOUR

1.   *who pray to God in bad French*: Voltaire used this derogatory phrase to refer to Huguenots; it was presumably familiar to the Catholic readers to whom his *Treatise* is addressed.

2.   *Jarnac, Moncontour, Coutras, Dreux, Saint-Denis*: These battles were fought, respectively, in 1569, 1569, 1587, 1562 and

1567 during the French wars of religion. Three of them concluded with Protestant defeats and two with victories for the Huguenots.

3.   *Sorbonne . . . Joan of Arc . . . Henry I V* : The Sorbonne's request to hand over Joan of Arc (*c.* 1412–31) to the Inquisition occurred in 1430. The same university announced the deposition of Henry IV in 1588.

4.   *Pope Sixtus V . . . against his sovereign*: In 1588 (rather than 1585), following the assassination of Cardinal de Guise, Sixtus V (1585–90) excommunicated Henry III and relieved his subjects of their obligation to obey him.

5.   *spill a king's blood*: Alludes to the execution of Charles I in 1649, which hardly resulted primarily from a religious dispute, as Voltaire claims.

6.   *Rapin-Thoiras*: Paul de Rapin de Thoyras (1661–1713) was a French Calvinist who emigrated after the revocation of the Edict of Nantes and joined the army of William of Orange (1650–1702). He fought in Ireland at the siege of Limerick and the Battle of the Boyne (1690) and subsequently wrote a ten-volume history of England, *Histoire de l'Angleterre* (The Hague, 1724–7), which was translated into English. Voltaire's summary of events in Ireland following the Irish Rebellion of 1641 was borrowed from news pamphlets that were printed in London and gave the impression that the atrocities committed in the Ulster rebellion were perpetrated only by the Catholic side.

7.   *The province . . . our kings*: The religious freedom of Protestants in Alsace was guaranteed by Sweden in the Treaty of Westphalia, which concluded the Thirty Years War (1618–48), rather than by any subsequent tolerant rule on the part of Louis XIV (1638–1715).

8.   *the Pretender*: Charles Edward Stuart, the Young Pretender (1720–88), the grandson of James II (1633–1701); in 1744 Voltaire had reported favourably to the Prussian ambassador that the French were providing him with a fleet to invade England against George II (1683–1760).

9.   *denied access to public offices*: The Test Act of 1673 (entitled 'An Act for preventing Dangers which may happen from Popish Recusants') barred Catholics and other non-conformists from appointment to public offices.

10.   *Anabaptist . . . Socinian*: Anabaptists rejected the practice of infant baptism and deferred the sacrament until the person

being baptized was mature enough to confess their faith. Socinians were named after Fausto Sozzini (1539–1604) and, in general, denied that the three persons of the Trinity shared the same divine nature or substance (consubstantiality).

11. *Jacobites, Nestorians and Monothelites ... Coptic rite ... Church of St John, Jews, Gebers and Banians*: Named after the sixth-century monk Jacob Baradaeus (d. 578), Jacobites denied that Christ had two natures (one human, the other divine); hence they were called monophysites or believers in one nature. Nestorians were named after a patriarch of Constantinople who was condemned at the Council of Ephesus (431) for teaching that there were two persons in Jesus Christ. Monothelites were condemned at the Third Council of Constantinople (680) because they believed that Jesus Christ had only one will. The Coptic Church separated from other Christian churches following a dispute about the theology of Christ and developed especially in Egypt. The Church of St John favoured a theology of Christ that was inspired by the fourth evangelist rather than by the Christology that St Paul developed in his epistles. Gebers or Guebres were followers of Zoroaster. Banians were Hindus.

12. *Yung-Chin ... expelled the Jesuits*: Emperor Yongzheng (or Yung-Chin) (1678–1735). The Jesuits were also expelled from France on two occasions, in 1575 and again in 1764.

13. *Edifying and Interesting Letters*: *Lettres édifiantes et curieuses écrites des missions étrangères* {Edifying and Interesting Letters written from Foreign Missions}, a collection of letters written by Jesuit missionaries in the Far East, was initially published in thirty-four volumes between 1703 and 1776; selections were subsequently translated into other European languages, including English. Extracts were read in Voltaire's school refectory when he was a pupil.

14. *the Catholic League and the Gunpowder Plot*: The Catholic League, a militant group founded in 1576 by Henry I, fought against Calvinists during the French religious wars of the sixteenth century. A group of English Catholics, inspired by local Jesuits and led by Robert Catesby and Guy Fawkes among others, planned to blow up the Parliament building in London on 5 November 1605 when James I was in attendance. The Gunpowder Plot was discovered in advance and its ringleaders were executed.

15. *the Jesuits arrived to add a thirteenth*: St Francis Xavier (1506–52), a founding member of the Jesuits, engaged in missionary work in Japan between 1549 and 1551.

16. *Minister Colbert*: Jean Baptiste Colbert (1619–83) was effectively minister for finance and commerce under Louis XIV. He focused on commercial developments and international trade to improve the financial stability of France, which had been impoverished by warfare.

17. *Carolina ... John Locke ... approves*: John Locke (1632–1704) drafted the Constitution of Carolina (1669), Article 97 of which provided that 'any seven or more persons agreeing in any religion, shall constitute a church or profession, to which they shall give some name, to distinguish it from others.' Voltaire's following comment rejecting Locke as a model for France reflects French opposition to Voltaire's glowing tributes to Locke in *Letters concerning the English Nation* (Letter 13).

18. *Philadelphia ... toleration*: Philadelphia was founded in 1681 by a Quaker, William Penn (1644–1718). Voltaire exaggerates the tolerant motivation for naming the city. The first four letters in *Letters concerning the English Nation* are devoted to the Quakers.

19. *mother who wants ... that he survives*: An allusion to the Judgement of Solomon, when two mothers claimed to have given birth to the same infant (I Kings/III Kings 3:16–27). Solomon identified the true mother as the woman who preferred to surrender the child rather than see him cut in two and shared equally between the women.

FIVE

1. *Molinists and Jansenists*: Luis de Molina (1535–1600) was a Spanish Jesuit who defended the doctrine that human beings are naturally free. Cornelius Jansen (1585–1638) was Bishop of Ypres; the posthumous publication of *Augustinus* (1640), his commentary on Augustine's theory of grace, initiated a reform movement within French Catholicism that emphasized the inability of human beings to act morally without divine grace. Molinists and Jansenists engaged in an acrimonious dispute about the necessity of grace for salvation and the alleged eternal damnation of those from whom God withheld sufficient grace.

2. *The more sects ... becomes*: Voltaire borrows this argument from Letter 6 of his *Letters concerning the English Nation* (On the Presbyterians), p. 41: 'If there were only one religion in

England there would be danger of despotism, if there were two they would cut each other's throats, but there are thirty, and they live in peace and happiness.'

3. *secure places for a particular sect*: One of the 'secret articles' of the Edict of Nantes (April 1598) allowed Huguenots to live in 'fortified places, towns and châteaux which they held up to the end of last August, in which there will be garrisons' for a period of eight years. The towns in question were predominantly Calvinist, such as La Rochelle, Montauban, Nîmes, etc.

4. *the minister ... unfortunate people*: Voltaire is specifically addressing the duc de Choiseul (1719–85), who was effectively prime minister and to whom Voltaire sent a copy of his *Treatise* in 1763.

5. *Saint-Médard ... are annihilated*: François de Pâris (1690–1727) was a deacon and supporter of Jansenism. After his death, hundreds of people visited his tomb in Paris and claimed to have been cured of diseases or to have witnessed other miracles while they experienced mystical convulsions there. These were known as the *convulsionnaires* of Saint-Médard. While they were tolerated in France, the campaign to eradicate Calvinism continued unabated against Huguenot pastors who were identified as 'prophets' or as engaged in a dedicated divine mission. Voltaire had discussed this issue under 'Convulsions' in his *Dictionnaire philosophique portatif*.

6. *Aristotle's categories, nature's abhorrence of a vacuum, quiddities, or to universals ... exemplified*: Voltaire refers to disputes between proponents of scholastic philosophy and its early modern critics. Aristotle's categories were a list of the ten most basic kinds of reality (e.g., a thing, a property, place, etc.). Scholastics argued against Blaise Pascal (1623–62) that mercury is supported in a Torricelli tube by nature's abhorrence of a vacuum, rather than by the weight of the atmosphere. A quiddity is the essence of something; and a universal is the assumed referent of general terms, such as 'justice'. The dispute hinged on whether only individual things exist (and universals are therefore mere abstractions) or whether universals also exist in the realities that exemplify them. During the seventeenth century the University of Paris and the *parlement* issued a number of decrees that banned the teaching of all philosophy except that of Aristotle.

7. *genuine sorcery and its imitations*: An allusion to trials for witchcraft and sorcery in France in the sixteenth and

seventeenth centuries, and to legal rules for conducting such trials or hearing appeals in the provincial *parlements*.

8. *excommunicate locusts ... rituals today*: Barthélemy de Chasseneuz reviews this practice in his *Consilium primum, de excommunicatione animalium insectorum* {Initial Advice about Excommunicating Insects} (Lyon, 1531). See E. P. Evans, *The Criminal Prosecution and Capital Punishment of Animals* (London: Heinemann, 1906), Ch. 1.

9. *Carpocratian, a Eutychian ... a Manichaean*: Carpocratians belonged to a Gnostic sect in the second century, and were often accused of libertinism. Eutychians were a fifth-century sect that disputed the doctrine of two natures in Christ. Manichaeans believed that there are twin sources of good and evil in the universe and were officially condemned by Christian churches because they appeared to deny the omnipotence of God. The other ancient sects are mentioned in Chapter 4, note 11.

10. *Le Tellier and Doucin ... sent it to Rome*: Michel Le Tellier (1643–1719) and Louis Doucin (1652–1726) were widely thought responsible for drafting the papal bull *Unigenitus* (1713) in which Pope Clement XI confirmed earlier papal condemnations of Jansenism.

11. *We now know its consequences*: Since a papal bull could not be implemented in France without being registered by provincial *parlements* and approved by French bishops, *Unigenitus* precipitated a lengthy dispute in France between opponents and supporters of the papal decision.

SIX

1. *the Malabar region*: The south-western coast of India.

SEVEN

1. *Trojans prayed ... the Greeks*: An allusion to Hecuba praying to the goddess Athena in the *Iliad*, VI. 294.

2. *He himself admitted ... simply ignorant*: In his *Apology* (21B–24B) Plato (*c.* 428–347 BC) summarizes how Socrates (469–399 BC) defended himself at his trial.

3. *A decent gentleman*: Jean Novi de Caveirac in his *Apologie* (see Chapter 4, note *, p. 23), pp. 375–6. The Phocian war

(356–346 BC) was allegedly fought because the Phocians were fined for cultivating sacred land.

EIGHT

1. *Pliny ... the Sun*: Pliny, *Natural History*, II. iv refers to the Sun as 'the soul, or more precisely the mind, of the whole world'.

2. *Cicero ... to believe that*: Here and in the following lines Voltaire quotes the Latin text loosely and then provides a French translation. The Cicero text is from *De natura deorum* (II. ii) {On the Nature of the Gods}.

3. *Juvenal ... believe it*: Juvenal, *Satires*, II. 152.

4. *There is nothing ... Death itself is nothing*: The chorus chants this in Seneca, *The Trojan Women*, line 397.

5. *Numa Pompilius*: A legendary second king of Rome who reigned *c.* 700 BC.

6. *Law of the Twelve Tables*: This ancient code included, in table ten, a number of prescriptions concerning religion.

7. *Josephus ... this story*: Flavius Josephus, a first-century historian, reports the story of Paulina in *The Antiquities of the Jews* (18.3).

8. *St James advised him ... law of Moses*: Acts 21:24: 'Take these and sanctify thyself with them: and bestow on them, that they may shave their heads. And all will know that the things which they have heard of thee are false: but that thou thyself also walkest keeping the law.'

9. *St Paul ... a Roman citizen*: Acts 7:58 reports that the witnesses to the stoning of St Stephen laid their cloaks at the feet of a young man whose name was Saul, who subsequently adopted the name Paul after his conversion to Christianity.

10. *Suetonius ... name of Christ*: The Roman historian Suetonius (*c.* 69–*c.* 150) wrote *De vita Caesarum* {Lives of the Caesars}. Voltaire quotes in Latin from Suetonius' Life of Claudius, xxv. 4.

11. *Dio Cassius*: Lucius Cassius Dio (*c.* 155–*c.* 235) was a Roman historian who wrote in Greek.

12. *Chinese ... their religion*: A reference to the massacre in 1740 of thousands of Chinese workers by Dutch troops in Jakarta, Indonesia, in what was then the Dutch East Indies.

NINE

1. *St Polyeuctus*: A soldier who was said to have been executed under emperor Valerian in 259 because he opposed the worship of false gods. Voltaire may have heard of him from Corneille's tragedy *Polyeucte*, which was first staged in 1641.

2. *The Christian . . . his sect*: Reported by Lactantius in *De Mortibus Persecutorum* {On the Deaths of Persecutors}, xiii. 2, and named Evethius in another early martyrology, this Christian allegedly tore down a public notice that announced Diocletian's orders to Christians to comply with the laws of the Empire. See Lactantius, *The Deaths of Persecutors*, ed. J. L. Creed (Oxford, 1984), pp. 20–21.

3. *Sacramentarians*: A term applied to various Christian sects which disputed the real presence of Christ in the Eucharist and instead believed in a spiritual or symbolic presence.

4. *Farel*: Guillaume Farel (1489–1565) was a French Christian reformer who was critical of the use of images in religious worship; he emigrated to Geneva, where he also encouraged Calvin to resettle.

5. *St Anthony the Hermit*: St Anthony (*c.* 468–*c.* 520) is generally regarded as one of the founders of the eremitical tradition in Western Christianity.

6. *Antinous*: Famously a beautiful youth, and a favourite of the emperor Hadrian, who drowned in the Nile; Hadrian later ranked Antinous as a god and had temples built in his honour.

7. *Tertullian*: *Apologetics*, Chapter 5.

8. *Lactantius . . . the Church*: Lactantius, *De Mortibus Persecutorum* {On the Deaths of Persecutors}, iv.

9. *Mr Dodwell*: Henry Dodwell (1641–1711) was a professor of history in Oxford who claimed in *Dissertationes Cyprianicae* {Cyprianic Dissertations} (Oxford, 1682) that the total number of martyrs in the early Church was much lower than had been believed. His views were challenged by Dom Thierry Ruinart (1657–1709) in *Acta primorum martyrum sincera et selecta* {The Sincere and Selected Acts of the First Martyrs} (1689).

10. *St Irenaeus . . . Telesphorus . . . put to death*: St Irenaeus (*c.* 130–*c.* 200) was bishop of what is now Lyon. There are references to Telesphorus in excerpts from his writings that survive in Eusebius, *Ecclesiastical History* (V. xxvi).

11. *Zephyrinus*: Pope Zephyrinus (*c.* 198–*c.* 217).

12. *Origen ... towns and villages*: Origen (*c.* 185–*c.* 254), a prolific Christian author from Alexandria, was regarded as unorthodox. The quotation is from *Contra Celsum* {Against Celsus}, III. viii.

13. *torn apart ... killed a cat*: This is not from Origen, but from a universal history written by Diodorus of Sicily (*c.* 90–*c.* 30 BC), *Bibliotheca historica* {Historical Library} (I. lxxxiii).

14. *St Gregory Thaumaturgus*: St Gregory (*c.* 213–70), named *Thaumaturgus* or the 'wonderworker', was born in Neocaesarea and was one of the first to have reported seeing a vision of Mary, the mother of Jesus.

15. *Shapur*: Shapur II (309–79) was one of the longest-serving emperors of the Sassanian Empire.

16. *Constantine*: The Roman Emperor Constantine the Great (*c.* 274–337).

17. *Theban Legion ... absurd fable*: A legion of Roman soldiers, based in Thebes, Egypt, was allegedly massacred in 286 for refusing to renounce their Christian faith.

18. *Verna Canopi*: 'A slave of Canopus'. Canopus was a city in lower Egypt; the word 'Canopus' was used to refer to that region and even to the whole of Egypt.

TEN

1. *The Sincere Acts ... depraved events*: See Chapter 9, note 9. Ruinart borrowed from a work by the Jesuit Jean Bolland (1596–1665) entitled *Acta sanctorum quotquot toto orbe coluntur* {Acts of All the Saints that Can Be Collected Worldwide}, which remained in print for more than two hundred years.

2. *Ancyra*: A city in Galatia in Roman times, and now Ankara in Turkey.

3. *St Romanus*: The martyrdom of St Romanus in 303 or 304 is reported by Eusebius in his *De martyribus Palaestinae* {History of the Martyrs in Palestine}, trans. W. Cureton (London, 1861), pp. 7–9.

4. *Sidrach, Misach and Abdenago ... furnace*: Daniel 3:26.

5. *St Romanus ... without a tongue*: *History of the Martyrs of Palestine* (p. 8); the story about Romanus still speaking fluently after his tongue is cut out was added by Ruinart.

6. *St Felicity*: There was a legend that St Felicity and her seven sons were martyred about the middle of the second century, but little else is recorded about her.

7. *Maccabees*: The martyrdom of the Maccabees is recounted in 2 Maccabees, Chapter 7 (which is not recognized as canonical by Protestant churches).

8. *St Hippolytus*: There was a Christian called St Hippolytus of Rome (*c.* 170–*c.* 235), but the story of his martyrdom probably resulted from the fact that his name was similar to that of Hippolytus, son of Theseus, whose death was associated with horses or chariots.

9. *the crucifix or the Bible*: Meaning Catholics or Protestants.

10. *Cévennes*: A range of mountains in south-central France where the Huguenot population (called *Camisards*) rebelled after the Edict of Nantes was revoked, and committed atrocities during the religious wars. These episodes lasted from 1702 to 1715.

11. *a drop of wine ... ignorant peasants*: Refers to Protestant celebrations of the Eucharist that differed from the Roman Catholic rite (in which only unleavened bread was used and consecrated wine was not given to the general public).

12. *the recent war*: The Seven Years War (1756–63), in which Britain and France were belligerents. The laws against Catholics and dissenters were not consistently implemented in England and Ireland during this period, but they remained on the statute books and were applied arbitrarily if needed.

13. *Newton had demonstrated*: Sir Isaac Newton's most famous work, *The Mathematical Principles of Natural Philosophy* (1687) revolutionized classical physics, but it was not generally accepted or taught in France until the middle of the eighteenth century. Voltaire and Mme du Châtelet were influential in making it known in France; Voltaire devoted a number of letters (14–17) to Newton in his *Letters concerning the English Nation* (1733) and published a lengthy introduction to Newton's physics, *Eléments de la philosophie de Newton* (1738).

14. *inoculation*: Voltaire contracted smallpox in 1723, during an outbreak in which he claimed 20,000 people died. Inoculation against the disease was introduced in England by Lady Mary Wortley Montagu (1689–1762), but the conservative medical establishment in France refused to follow this example. Voltaire discussed this in Letter 11 of his *Letters concerning the English Nation*.

15. *Varazze … Golden Legends*: Giacomo (or Jacopo) da Varazze (1228–98) was a Dominican friar who became Archbishop of Genoa. He composed hagiographies of saints in a Latin collection entitled *Legenda aurea* {Golden Legends}.

16. *Ribadeneira … Flower of the Saints*: Pedro de Ribadeneira (1527–1611), one of the earliest Jesuits, composed lives of the saints under the title *Flos Sanctorum* {Flower of the Saints}.

ELEVEN

1. *Cardinal Duperron … suppression*: Jacques Duperron (1556–1618) converted from Protestantism and was eventually made a Roman Catholic cardinal. He opposed the decision of the *parlement* in Paris that the king's civil powers were not subject to the Pope and persuaded the regent, Marie de' Medici, not to implement it.

2. *My Father is greater than me*: John 14:28.

3. *Councils of Nicaea and Constantinople … Eusebius of Nicomedia*: The First Council of Nicaea (325) decided, against Arius (and Arianism), that Jesus Christ was God and it summarized its doctrine in the 'Nicene Creed'. Eusebius of Nicomedia subsequently attempted to qualify the condemnation of Arianism, which was confirmed at the First Council of Constantinople in 381.

4. *Ratramnus … Paschasius Radbertus … Berengarius … Scotus*: An allusion to disputes about the theology of the Eucharist. Ratramnus (d. *c.* 870), who was abbot of Corbie in northern France, defended a spiritualist interpretation of Christ's words 'This is my body' in *De corpore et sanguine Domini* {On the Body and Blood of the Lord}. Paschasius Radbertus (785–865), who was also abbot of the same monastery for a time, defended a realist interpretation of the same words in his *De corpore et sanguine Domini*. When Berengarius of Tours (*c.* 999–1088) adopted the interpretation of Ratramnus, he was condemned by the Council of Vercelli (1050) and later signed an official renunciation of the condemned doctrine at the Roman Council (1079). That ninth-century dispute anticipated similar disputes about the theology of the Eucharist between Catholic and Reformed churches in France in Voltaire's time. John Scotus Eriugena (*c.* 810–*c.* 877), an Irish philosopher, also proposed a theology of the Eucharist closer to that of Ratramnus; he taught that the body of Christ is present in the Eucharist only symbolically or spiritually.

5. *Holy Spirit . . . God the Father . . . God the Son*: The appropriate way to describe the relationships within the Trinity between the Father, the Son and the Holy Spirit was disputed in the early centuries of Christianity. The Holy Spirit was initially said to 'proceed' only from the Father, but subsequently it was decided that the Holy Spirit proceeded from both the Father and the Son, since both of them were equally God.

6. *Honorius I*: Pope Honorius I (d. 638) taught that Jesus Christ had only one will, rather than a divine and a human will. His views were condemned officially by the Third Council of Constantinople in 680 (see above on Monothelites, Chapter 4, note 11).

7. *Immaculate Conception*: The belief that the mother of Jesus Christ was born without original sin developed in the Latin Church during the Middle Ages, and was taught officially by Pope Sixtus IV in 1476 and by the Council of Trent in 1546. In 1854 Pope Pius IX defined it as a dogma of faith.

8. *Cephas*: An alternative name for Peter, who had been renamed 'the Rock' by Christ.

9. *But when I saw . . . the Jews*: I quote the Vulgate version of Galatians 2:14, rather than Voltaire's translation of the text.

10. *that very period*: i.e., the first decades of Christianity.

11. *St Matthew . . . St Luke . . . different*: Matthew 1:1–16; Luke 3:23–8.

12. *St Paul . . . justify anyone*: Romans 3:28: 'For we account a man to be justified by faith, without the works of the law.'

13. *St James . . . without works*: James 2:26: 'For even as the body without the spirit is dead: so also faith without works is dead.'

TWELVE

1. *God commanded . . . the Passover*: Exodus 12:3–11.

2. *He commanded . . . right foot*: Leviticus 8:23.

3. *God ordered . . . Hazazel*: Leviticus 16:21.

4. *This prince . . . the temple*: 2 Paralipomenon (2 Chronicles) 4:3.

5. *Roboam . . . pontiff*: 1 Kings (3 Kings) 12:28.

6. *The small kingdom . . . Roboam's reign*: 2 Paralipomenon (2 Chronicles) 11:17, 12:1–12.

7. *The holy king . . . high places*: 2 Paralipomenon (2 Chronicles) 15:17.

8. *Out of the sixteen . . . thirty-two souls*: Numbers 31:40.

9. *Ôtô tîrasch*: Voltaire quotes the Latin phrase of the Vulgate, *tibi iure debentur*, and then gives the corresponding phrase in Hebrew, which he had requested from a correspondent who was able to read the original text of Judges 11:24.

10. *He punished the Philistines . . . idolatry*: 1 Samuel (1 Kings) 6.

11. *The severity . . . own reason*: Voltaire quotes from Antoine Augustin Calmet's *Commentaire littéral sur tous les livres de l'Ancien et du Nouveau Testament* {A Literal Commentary on all the Books of the Old and New Testaments}, III, 371 with a minor amendment.

12. *The riches . . . less surprising*: Herodotus, *Histories*, Book I.

13. *in Malachi . . . pure oblations*: Malachi 1:11.

THIRTEEN

1. *Honour thy father . . . the land*: Deuteronomy 5:16.

2. *Warburton*: William Warburton (1698–1779) argues in *The Divine Legation of Moses, demonstrated on the Principles of a Religious Deist* (3nd edn, London, 1742) that God's failure to mention an afterlife in His revelation to Moses confirms His authorship of the Decalogue, because, paradoxically, He alone knew the truth well enough to conceal part of it.

3. *the Synagogue . . . St Jerome tells us*: In the prologue to St Jerome's commentary on Ezechiel, *Commentariorum in Hiezechielem, libri xiv*.

4. *the Synagogue did not allow . . . with Moses*: Voltaire discussed this passage from Ezechiel, and the prohibition on young readers, in the article entitled 'Ezechiel' in the *Dictionnaire philosophique portatif*.

FOURTEEN

1. *These words . . . much abused*: Pierre Bayle (1647–1706) wrote a multi-volume commentary on the phrase 'compel them to come in', *Commentaire philosophique* (1686–8), from which Voltaire borrows.

2. *the merchants . . . unclean animals*: Mark 11:15 and Matthew 8:30–32.

3. *the father of a family . . . water into wine*: Luke 15:1–32; Matthew 20:6–16; Luke 10:30–37; Matthew 9:14–15; Luke 7:-37–48; John 8:3–11; John 2:2–9.

4. *He does not even get angry . . . with lodging*: Matthew 26:21;
    Matthew 26:51-2; Luke 9:54-5.

5. *The lawgiver for Christians . . . forgive his enemies*: Luke
    23:34.

6. *I adjure thee . . . Son of God*: Matthew 26:63.

7. *son of Belial*: 1 Samuel (1 Kings) 25:17.

8. *Thou hast said it . . . clouds of Heaven*: Matthew 26:64.

9. *what we learn from Josephus*: Josephus, *Jewish Antiquities*,
    XVIII. iii.

10. *Pilate did not . . . displayed later*: See Chapter 8, p. 40 above,
    and Acts 25:16.

FIFTEEN

1. *Witnesses against Intolerance*: Voltaire borrowed all of these
    citations from two contemporary sources. Seventeen come from
    Antoine Court, *Le Patriote français et impartial* {The Impartial
    French Patriot} (Lausanne, 1751), while the remaining five are
    borrowed from Chevalier de Beaumont, *L'Accord parfait de la
    nature, de la raison, de la révélation et de la politique* {The
    Perfect Agreement of Nature, Reason, Revelation and Politics}
    (Cologne, 1753). See Anne-Marie Mercier-Faivre, 'Le *Traité sur
    la tolérance*, tolérance et réécriture', in *Etudes sur la Traité sur
    la tolérance de Voltaire*, ed. Nicholas Cronk (Oxford: Voltaire
    Foundation, 2000), pp. 34–55.

2. *Apology, Chap. 24*: Tertullian, *Apology on Behalf of Chris-
    tians*, xxiv (p. 81).

3. *Lactantius, Book 3*: Incorrect reference. Lactantius, *Divine
    Institutes*, V. xix–xx, expresses these sentiments, but not liter-
    ally as Voltaire reports.

4. *Tillemont, Ecclesiastical History, Vol. 6*: Louis-Sébastien Le
    Nain de Tillemont (1637–98), author of *Mémoires pour servir à
    l'histoire ecclésiastique des six premiers siècles* {Memoirs for
    Use as an Ecclesiastical History of the First Six Centuries}.

5. *De Thou, Letter of Dedication to Henry IV*: See Chapter 3,
    note *, p. 19, for the book by De Thou in which this dedication
    occurs.

6. *Montesquieu, The Spirit of the Laws, Book 25*: De l'esprit des
    lois, XXV. xiii.

SIXTEEN

1. *sign this document . . . have ever read*: Alludes to the formulary that Jansenist supporters were forced to sign in the seventeenth century, which identified five propositions that were allegedly found in Jansen's *Augustinus*. Rome condemned the propositions as heretical, but Jansenists denied that the propositions were even in the book.

2. *Lanfranc against Berengarius*: Lanfranc (1005–89), Archbishop of Canterbury, defended the traditional doctrine of transubstantiation against the spiritual or symbolic presence that was proposed by Berengarius (see Chapter 11, note 4).

3. *St Thomas against St Bonaventure*: St Thomas Aquinas (1225–74) was a member of the Dominican order, while St Bonaventure (1221–74) was a Franciscan. Although Voltaire does not specify any particular issue on which they differed, the two mendicant orders disagreed about many doctrinal questions.

4. *Second Council of Nicaea . . . Council of Frankfurt*: The Second Council of Nicaea (787) and the Council of Frankfurt (794) issued opposing decrees concerning the use of images in religious celebrations. Voltaire discussed the same issue in his *Dictionnaire philosophique portatif*, under 'Councils'.

5. *My Father . . . as great as Him*: John 14:28 includes the phrase 'the Father is greater than me'; nonetheless, the official teaching of the Church was that Christ was the Son of God and was co-equal with the Father.

6. *the homage that vice pays to virtue*: La Rochefoucauld (1613–80), *Maxims*, No. 218. Those who failed to profess allegiance to the Catholic Church were denied burial in consecrated ground – a fate that almost befell Voltaire. After his death his friends had to dress his corpse as if he were still alive and smuggle it out of Paris for burial in the Abbey of Scellières, where it remained until reburial in the Panthéon in 1791.

SEVENTEEN

1. *Le Tellier*: Michel Le Tellier (1642–1719) had taught in the Jesuit college of Louis-le-Grand for twenty-eight years (where Voltaire had been educated) and was the Provincial Superior of the Jesuits in 1709. As confessor to Louis XIV, he was believed

to have influenced the king to implement the Jesuits' anti-Jansenist campaign, and to have been partly responsible for the papal condemnation of Jansenism in the bull *Unigenitus*.

2. *if we are obliged ... must be killed*: St Thomas Aquinas argues (in the *Summa theologiae*, IIaIIae, Q. 11, art. 3) that heretics may be killed to prevent them from corrupting the faith of Christian believers.

3. *most recent war*: An allusion to the War of the Spanish Succession (1701–13).

4. *Sanchez and Molina*: Voltaire often mocked the Jesuit Thomás Sanchez (1550–1610) because of his authorship of a book on marriage, *Disputationes de sancti matrimonii sacramento* {Disputations concerning the Sacrament of Holy Matrimony} (Madrid, 1605). On Molina, see Chapter 5, note 1.

5. *Battle of Höchstädt*: A reference to the second Battle of Höchstädt, also known as the Battle of Blenheim (13 August 1704), at which the army of Louis XIV (1638–1715) suffered heavy casualties.

6. *the monk Schwartz ... pulvis pyrius*: In the eighteenth century Berthold Schwartz was widely believed to have invented gunpowder, but it is unclear if such an historical individual ever existed.

7. *Cardinal de Noailles*: (1651–1729) A staunch defender of the independence of the French Church; he refused to endorse the bull *Unigenitus*, which condemned Jansenism.

8. *Emperor Henry VII*: The Holy Roman Emperor Henry VII (1275–1313) allegedly died when someone introduced poison into the consecrated wine used in the Eucharist.

9. *Molinists*: See Chapter 5, note 1.

10. *if we cause their death ... their heavenly joy*: Voltaire alludes to the doctrine of 'directing the intention', which had been criticized trenchantly by Pascal in his *Lettres provinciales* {Provincial Letters}. According to this doctrine, which Pascal attributed to the Jesuits, an evil action could be turned into a morally permissible action by modifying the intention with which the agent performs it.

11. *1707*: This probably refers to the outbreak of controversy when Clement XI condemned Jansenism in *Universi dominici gregis* (July 1708).

12. *A native of Angoulême*: An allusion to Ravaillac. See Chapter 1, note 5.

13. *the following year*: Le Tellier was exiled in 1715.

EIGHTEEN

1. *the Oratory*: A religious congregation of priests that was introduced into France in 1611 by Pierre de Bérulle (1575–1629). The Oratorians founded many colleges in competition with those of the Jesuits and were sympathetic to Jansenist theology.
2. *Quesnel*: Pasquier Quesnel (1634–1719) was a member of the Oratory and one of the most prominent defenders of Jansenism.
3. *Jesuits complain ... the Church*: The Jesuits were expelled from France on two occasions, the second of which was in 1762 (although the decision was registered by the *parlement* in 1764). See Additional Chapter, note 4.
4. *We follow the guidance ... rather than men*: Acts 5:29. Appealing to conscience and refusing to recognize the jurisdiction of 'heretical' princes was characteristic of Calvinist political theory in the sixteenth century among authors such as Théodore de Bèze (1519–1605), François Hotman (1524–90) and Philippe Du Plessis-Mornay (1549–1623).
5. *a small sect in Denmark ... to Heaven*: Voltaire discussed the same sect in his *Dictionnaire philosophique portatif*, under 'Baptism'.
6. *Hethites, Jebusites ... subject to a curse*: Voltaire lists descendants of Chanaan from Genesis 10:15–18.

NINETEEN

1. *Confucius*: The Chinese philosopher Confucius (551–479 BC). See Chapter 22, note 8.

TWENTY

1. *A rational, violent and powerful atheist ... superstitious person*: The idea that any religion, no matter how superstitious, is better than none because it restrains human behaviour was defended by Jean Bodin in various works; see, for example, *Colloque de Jean Bodin des secrets cachez des choses sublimes*: *Colloquium of the Seven about Secrets of the Sublime*, trans. M. L. Daniels Kuntz (Princeton: Princeton University Press, 1975), p. 162.
2. *St Genou cured ... St Clare healed diseased eyes*: The cult of St Genou developed in the early Middle Ages and became associated

with a basilica in the region formerly known as Berry in the Loire Valley. It is unclear if there was any historical person of that name, which has survived in the town of Saint-Genouph in the Indre-et-Loire department. St Clare (*c.* 1193–1253) was a disciple of St Francis of Assisi and founder of the enclosed religious order of nuns known as the Poor Clares.

3. *M. de Noailles, the bishop of Châlons . . . against him*: A reference to Gaston-Jean-Baptiste-Louis de Noailles, the brother of Cardinal de Noailles, and an episode in 1702 that Voltaire recounts in *The Age of Louis XIV* (Ch. 35).

4. *the authors of the Life of St Francis Xavier . . . returned it to him*: Among the biographers of St Francis Xavier, Voltaire identified Dominique Bouhours (1628–1702), *Vie de S. François Xavier, apôtre des Indes et du Japon* {The Life of St Francis Xavier, Apostle of the Indies and Japan} (Paris: S. Mabre-Cramoisy, 1682).

5. *Pope Gregory V . . . with a goose*: Robert II (971–1031) divorced his wife to marry his cousin Bertha. Pope Gregory V objected that it was in breach of canon law, because they were related within the degrees of consanguinity that were forbidden for marriage.

6. *convulsionaries . . . the population*: See above Chapter 5, note 5, and the article on 'Convulsions' in the *Dictionnaire philosophique portatif*.

7. *Pascal . . . Fontenelle*: Some well-known French intellectuals of the seventeenth century. Blaise Pascal (1623–62), Pierre Nicole (1625–95) and Antoine Arnauld (1612–94) were prominent supporters of Jansenism; René Descartes (1596–1650) and Pierre Gassendi (1592–1655) were philosophers, while Jacques-Bénigne Bossuet (1627–1704), Pierre Bayle (1647–1706) and Bernard le Bovier de Fontenelle (1657–1757) were theologians.

8. *Garasse and Menot*: François Garasse (1585–1631) was a Jesuit author who published extremely partisan defences of the Catholic religion, e.g., *La Doctrine curieuse des beaux esprits de ce temps ou prétendus tels* {The Strange Doctrine of the Great Minds of our Era, or Those Who Claim to be Such} (Paris, 1623). But contrary to the impression given by Voltaire, Garasse was a contemporary of Descartes, Gassendi and others who represented 'reason'. Michel Menot (+ 1518) was a Franciscan friar who was famous for his preaching.

9. *a seed must rot in order to germinate*: Alludes to 1 Corinthians 15:36: 'Senseless man, that which thou sowest is not quickened, except it die first.'

10. *stupid*: Voltaire uses the French word *bête*, which is also the word for an animal. The phrase used in the subsequent sentence is 'bêtes farouches', which has connotations of a wild beast.

11. *from across the Alps*: Voltaire's use of the word *ultramontane* alludes to the independence from Rome that the Church in France claimed, or in this case the detrimental effects of superstitions that originated in Italy.

TWENTY-ONE

1. *Bishop Alexander ... cannot possibly understand*: Alexander and Arius disputed a theological opinion that became known, following its condemnation by the Council of Nicaea, as the Arian heresy. Eusebius of Caesarea (*c.* 260–*c.* 340) wrote a *Life of Constantine* in which the Emperor's advice to the disputing parties is reported in Bk II, Ch. 69. Socrates Scolasticus (*c.* 380–*c.* 450) reported Constantine's advice in his *Ecclesiastical History*, I. vii.

2. *the homoousion ... cutting your throats*: The controversy about whether Jesus Christ had the same nature as God the Father or had a similar nature was reflected in the two Greek words for 'same nature' and 'similar nature' (*homoousion* and *homoiousion*). The term 'hypostasis' was translated in Trinitarian theology as 'person', to distinguish within a unique God three different expressions of the Divinity.

3. *Archimedes or Posidonius or Varro or Cato or Cicero ... replied*: Apart from Archimedes (*c.* 287–212), the other ancient authors mentioned were all associated with Stoicism. Posidonius of Rhodes (135–51 BC) was a mathematician; Marcus Terentius Varro (116–27 BC) and Marcus Porcius Cato Uticensis or Cato the Younger (95–46 BC) were also Stoic sympathizers. Marcus Tullius Cicero (106–43 BC) was a Roman politician, rhetorician and one of the most important ancient Latin authors whose influence on the development of the Latin language was without equal.

4. *He may have been flattered ... with gems*: Alludes to Constantine presiding over the Council of Nicaea, which he summoned in 325.

TWENTY-TWO

1. *The Academy of Crusca*: Voltaire was an elected member of this academy, which produced a standard dictionary of Italian in 1612.

2. *the grammar of Buonmattei*: Benedetto Buonmattei (1581–1647) was a member of the Academy of Crusca, which published a revised edition of his grammar of Tuscan Italian, *Della lingua toscana due libri* {Two Books concerning the Tuscan Language} (Florence, 1760).

3. *Father Ivonet ... Gambellinus*: This list of unfamiliar names is borrowed from Morellet's *Manual* about people who acted as judges of the Inquisition in the fourteenth century. Some of the names were either misspelled or corrupted, and I have substituted names that correspond to historically identifiable people where possible.

4. *Outside the Church there is no salvation*: The Roman Catholic Church taught consistently, throughout the centuries, that membership of the Church was a necessary condition for salvation and that all those who were not members were eternally damned. This doctrine was formally announced, for example, in the Profession of Faith issued by Pope Pius IV (13 November 1564), following the Council of Trent; in Voltaire's day, Pope Benedict XIV (16 March 1743) repeated the same teaching when he identified the Catholic Church as the one true church, 'extra quam nemo salvus esse potest' {outside of which no one can be saved}.

5. *Love God and your neighbour*: Luke 10:27.

6. *one letter of the alphabet*: See Chapter 21, note 2; there was only a difference of one letter ('i') in the Greek descriptions of the disputed doctrines in the Arian controversy.

7. *omission of a few words ... have known about*: An allusion to the belief that the few words used in the ceremony of baptism and pouring ordinary water over someone's head would save an individual from eternal damnation.

8. *Confucius ... model human beings*: Voltaire lists a number of pagans who were almost universally acknowledged as outstanding human beings. Apart from Confucius, Socrates and Plato, whom he has mentioned earlier, he includes the Greek legislator Solon (*c.* 628–*c.* 558 BC), the Greek philosopher and mathematician Pythagoras (570–490 BC); Zaleucus (seventh century BC), who is reputed to have compiled the first Greek code of law; three Roman emperors, Antoninus Pius (86–161), Trajan (53–117) and Titus (39–81), and the Greek Stoic philosopher Epictetus (55–135), whose main writings were the *Discourses*.

9. *Jean Châtel, Ravaillac, Damiens, Cartouche*: Jean Châtel (1575–94) was executed at the age of nineteen for having attempted to

assassinate Henry IV, while one of his Jesuit teachers, Father Guignard (who taught at the Jesuit Clermont College, where Voltaire was educated, after a change in its name) was also executed for his complicity in the crime. For Ravaillac, see Chapter 1, note 5. Robert-François Damiens (1715–57) was executed for an attempt on the life of Louis XV (1710–74). Louis-Dominique Cartouche (1693–1721) was also a former student of the Jesuit College in Paris and was executed for robbery.

TWENTY-FOUR

1. *This author . . . The Harmony of Religion and Humanity*: Pierre-Claude Malvaux, *L'Accord de la religion et de l'humanité* (Paris: Desprez, 1762), which was published one year before Voltaire's essay.

2. *Bishop of Hippo*: St Augustine.

3. *If one wishes . . . their virtues*: Molière, *Les Femmes savantes* (Act I, Scene 1, ll. 72–3).

4. *That is what he suggests*: Malvaux is not quite so explicit, and recommends the harshest treatment for those who lead unfortunate people into heresy.

5. *Bayle among the supporters of intolerance*: Pierre Bayle (1647–1706), the author of the *Dictionnaire historique et critique* {An Historical and Critical Dictionary}, which appeared originally in 1697 and subsequently in many further editions. Bayle, a French Calvinist living in the United Provinces, was a renowned defender of religious toleration.

6. *Defence of the St Bartholomew's Day Massacre*: Voltaire compares Malvaux with Novi de Caveirac (see Chapter 4, footnote *, p. 23).

7. *Dauphiny . . . Carcassonne*: There were significant Huguenot communities in these regions, towns and villages.

8. *receive communion . . . to have children*: Refers to Catholics, who usually received communion only in the form of a wafer, rather than also in the form of wine. The Council of Trent used the term 'species' to describe either form of the sacrament, because it taught that after the consecration of the Mass what appeared to be bread or wine was not such.

9. *our author*: Pierre-Claude Malvaux, *L'Accord*, II. iii. article 2.

10. *Count d'Avaux*: Jean-Antoine de Mesmes, Count of Avaux (1640–1709), was French ambassador to the United Provinces,

and recorded his memoirs as *Négociations de M. le comte d'Avaux en Hollande, despuis 1679 jusqu'en 1684*, 6 vols. (Paris: Durand, 1752–3). Louis XIV's reply was dated 18 October 1685.

11. *Pellison ... accomplice of Fouquet*: Paul Pellison-Fontanier (1624–93) served under Nicolas Fouquet (1615–80), who had been Superintendant of Finances until Louis XIV dismissed him. Fouquet was imprisoned in the Bastille until his death, whereas Pellison converted to Catholicism, regained the favour of the king and published various religious booklets and a history of the Académie française.

12. *A Marshal of France*: A reference to Louis-François-Armand de Vignerot du Plessis de Richelieu (1696–1788), who had been named a 'Marshal of France' by Louis XIV and did not support the dragooning of troops on Huguenot lands as a form of punishment.

13. *the three twentieths*: The meaning is unclear, since it fails to match the fractions of population mentioned in the text.

TWENTY-FIVE

1. *The Chancellor*: Guillaume de Lamoignon de Blancmesnil (1683–1772).

2. *Mr de Crosne*: Louis Thiroux de Crosne (1736–94), who later became lieutenant general of police in 1785 and was guillotined during the French Revolution.

3. *Provincial Letters*: Pascal published these letters anonymously, one by one, between January 1656 and March 1657; they were then collected and published in Paris in 1657.

4. *One could print tracts ... their decision*: Here Voltaire deleted nine short paragraphs in which he commented on the use in French criminal justice of rules for adding together items of evidence that are not individually probative to generate sufficient evidence for conviction.

5. *There is a very large edifice ... my own hands*: Probably refers to the simplicity of the Church as founded by Christ, in contrast with the accretions that were added over the centuries by theologians.

AN ADDITIONAL CHAPTER

1. *An Account of the Most Recent Decision in Favour of the Calas Family*: This Appendix was added in the edition of the *Nouveaux Mélanges* (1765).

2. *the final judgement*: This was issued on 9 March 1765.

3. *use of receipts for confession . . . to hate them*: Catholics were required to confess at least once a year at Easter and, since it was difficult to distinguish practising Catholics from others, some priests instituted a system of providing a receipt to confirm that an individual had complied with their annual duty. Those who failed to produce such a receipt were denied the sacraments of the dying and were denied burial in consecrated ground. The same requirement was later used against Jansenists who refused to sign the formulary. See Chapter 16, note 1.

4. *A major bankruptcy . . . the last straw*: Antoine La Valette (1708–67), a Jesuit priest who worked on the missions in Martinique, was involved in major commercial activities that went bankrupt; the Jesuit order was held responsible for his debts in 1761 and the Paris *parlement* subsequently decided to disband the order in France and in French territories.

5. *The Destruction of the Jesuits in France . . . written by a philosopher*: Jean le Rond d'Alembert (1717–83), *Sur la destruction des Jésuites en France. Par un auteur désintéressé* (1765).

6. *misled great minds*: In Letter 25 of the *Letters concerning the English Nation* Voltaire acknowledged that he respected 'the genius and the eloquence of Pascal', but he disagreed fundamentally with the 'eloquent fallacies and admirably argued falsehoods' that were implied by Pascal's notes, which were published posthumously under the title *Pensées* (1670).

7. *Mr de Beaumont*: Jean-Baptiste-Jacques Élie de Beaumont, *Mémoire à consulter et consultation pour les enfants du défunt Jean Calas, marchand à Toulouse* {A Memoir to be Consulted, and a Submission on behalf of the Children of the Deceased Jean Calas, a Merchant at Toulouse} (Paris: Merlin, 1765).

8. *Mr de Bacquencourt*: Guillaume-Joseph Dupleix, Lord of Bacquencourt (1727–94), was responsible for drafting the final submission to the full court.

9. *the king . . . granted him*: Louis XV was known as *Louis le bien aimé* {Louis the Beloved}.

PENGUIN CLASSICS

THE RETURN OF THE NATIVE
THOMAS HARDY

> 'You are ambitious, Eustacia – no not exactly ambitious, luxurious.
> I ought to be of the same vein, to make you happy, I suppose'

Tempestuous Eustacia Vye passes her days dreaming of passionate love and
the escape it may bring from the small community of Egdon Heath. Hearing
that Clym Yeobright is to return from Paris, she sets her heart on marrying him,
believing that through him she can leave rural life and find fulfilment elsewhere.
But she is to be disappointed, for Clym has dreams of his own, and they have little
in common with Eustacia's. Their unhappy marriage causes havoc in the lives
of those close to them, in particular Damon Wildeve, Eustacia's former lover,
Clym's mother and his cousin Thomasin. *The Return of the Native* illustrates the
tragic potential of romantic illusion and how its protagonists fail to recognize their
opportunities to control their own destinies.

Penny Boumelha's introduction examines the classical and mythological references
and the interplay of class and sexuality in the novel. This edition, essentially
Hardy's original book version of the novel, also includes notes, a glossary,
chronology and bibliography.

Edited with notes by Tony Slade and an introduction by Penny Boumelha

Penguin Classics

THE PRIVATE MEMOIRS AND CONFESSIONS OF A JUSTIFIED SINNER JAMES HOGG

> 'My life has been a life of trouble and turmoil; of change and vicissitude;
> of anger and exultation; of sorrow and of vengeance'

Robert Colwan, a clergyman's son, is so confident of his salvation as one of the Lord's elect that he comes to look on himself as a man apart, unhindered by considerations of mere earthly law. Through Robert's own unforgettable account, we follow the strange and sinful life into which he is led by a devilish doppelgänger – a life that will finally lead him to murder. Steeped in the folkloric superstitions and theological traditions of eighteenth-century Scotland, this macabre and haunting novel is a devastating portrayal of the stages by which the human spirit can descend into darkness.

Based on the first edition of 1824, John Wain's text incorporates key revisions from the 1837 edition to provide the most accurate possible version of this complex and rewarding work. In his introduction, he illuminates the novel's historical background of religious and political controversy.

'Astounding' André Gide

Edited with an introduction by John Wain

PENGUIN CLASSICS

DIALOGUES CONCERNING NATURAL RELIGION
DAVID HUME

'Were this world ever so perfect a production, it must still remain uncertain, whether all the excellences of the work can justly be ascribed to the workman'

In the posthumously published *Dialogues Concerning Natural Religion*, the Enlightenment philosopher David Hume attacked many of the traditional arguments for the existence of God, expressing the belief that religion is founded on ignorance and irrational fears. Though calm and courteous in tone – at times even tactfully ambiguous – the conversations between Hume's vividly realized fictional figures form perhaps the most searching case ever mounted against orthodox Christian theological thinking and the 'deism' of the time, which pointed to the wonders of creation as conclusive evidence of God's Design. Hume's characters debate these issues with extraordinary passion, lucidity and humour, in one of the most compelling philosophical works ever written.

Based on Hume's own manuscript, Martin Bell provides an accessible modern edition, while his fascinating introduction sets Hume's religious scepticism in the philosophical and scientific context of its time.

Edited with an introduction by Martin Bell

PENGUIN CLASSICS

ON LIBERTY
JOHN STUART MILL

'The only freedom which deserves the name
is that of pursuing our own good in our own way'

On Liberty is dedicated to one simple principle: that men and women should be free to do as they please, without interference from society or the State, unless their actions might cause harm to others. While many of his immediate predecessors and contemporaries, from Adam Smith to William Godwin and Thoreau, had celebrated liberty, it was Mill who transformed the concept into a philosophy, claiming for it a central role in social policy and government and arguing for a redrawing of the line between the authority wielded by the State and the independence of the individual – a view that continues to inform debates about personal liberty to this day.

This edition contains an introduction, which puts the work in its biographical and political context, and explores the unresolved contradictions in liberal philosophy.

Edited with an introduction by Gertrude Himmelfarb

PENGUIN CLASSICS

THE LIFE OF SAMUEL JOHNSON
JAMES BOSWELL

> **'Johnson, to be sure, has a roughness in his manner,
> but no man alive has a more tender heart'**

In Boswell's *Life of Samuel Johnson*, one of the towering figures of English literature is revealed with unparalleled immediacy and originality, in a biography to which we owe much of our knowledge of the man himself. Through a series of richly detailed anecdotes, Johnson emerges as a sociable figure, vigorously engaging and fencing with great contemporaries such as Garrick, Goldsmith, Burney and Burke, and of course with Boswell himself. Yet anxieties and obsessions also darkened Johnson's private hours, and Boswell's attentiveness to every facet of Johnson's character makes this biography as moving as it is entertaining.

In this entirely new and unabridged edition, David Womersley's introduction examines the motives behind Boswell's work, and the differences between the two men that drew them to each other. It also contains chronologies of Boswell and Johnson, appendices and comprehensive indexes, including biographical details.

Edited with notes and an introduction by David Womersley

Penguin Classics

CRITIQUE OF PURE REASON
IMMANUEL KANT

'In order to know an object, I must be able to prove its possibility, either from its actuality, as attested by experience, or a priori, by means of reason'

Kant's *Critique of Pure Reason* (1781) is the central text of modern philosophy. It brings together the two opposing schools of philosophy: rationalism, which grounds all our knowledge in reason, and empiricism, which traces all our knowledge to experience. The *Critique* is a profound and challenging investigation into the nature of human reason, establishing its truth and its falsities, its illusions and its reality. Reason, argues Kant, is the seat of all concepts, including God, freedom and immortality, and must therefore precede and surpass human experience.

Marcus Weigelt's lucid re-working of Max Muller's classic translation makes the work accessible to a new generation of readers. His informative introduction places the work in context and elucidates Kant's main arguments. This edition also contains a bibliography and notes.

Translated with an introduction by Marcus Weigelt

PENGUIN CLASSICS

BEYOND GOOD AND EVIL
FRIEDRICH NIETZSCHE

'That which is done out of love always takes place beyond good and evil'

Beyond Good and Evil confirmed Nietzsche's position as the towering European philosopher of his age. The work dramatically rejects the tradition of Western thought with its notions of truth and God, good and evil. Nietzsche demonstrates that the Christian world is steeped in a false piety and infected with a 'slave morality'. With wit and energy, he turns from this critique to a philosophy that celebrates the present and demands that the individual imposes their own 'will to power' upon the world.

This edition includes a commentary on the text by the translator and an introduction by Michael Tanner, which explains some of the more abstract passages in *Beyond Good and Evil*.

'One of the greatest books of a very great thinker' Michael Tanner

Translated by R. J. Hollingdale with an introduction by Michael Tanner

Penguin Classics

PENSÉES
BLAISE PASCAL

> 'If we submit everything to reason our religion
> will be left with nothing mysterious or supernatural'

Blaise Pascal, the precociously brilliant contemporary of Descartes, was a gifted mathematician and physicist, but it is his unfinished apologia for the Christian religion upon which his reputation now rests. The *Pensées* is a collection of philosophical fragments, notes and essays in which Pascal explores the contradictions of human nature in psychological, social, metaphysical and – above all – theological terms. Mankind emerges from Pascal's analysis as a wretched and desolate creature within an impersonal universe, but who can be transformed through faith in God's grace.

This masterly translation by A. J. Krailsheimer conveys Pascal's disarmingly personal tone and captures all the fire and passion of the original. Also contained in this volume are a comparison between different editions, appendices and a bibliography.

Translated with an introduction by A. J. Krailsheimer

PENGUIN CLASSICS

CONVERSATIONS OF SOCRATES
XENOPHON

Socrates' Defence/Memoirs of Socrates/The Estate-Manager/The Dinner-Party

'He seemed to me to be the perfect example of goodness and happiness'

After the execution of Socrates in 399 BC, a number of his followers wrote dialogues featuring him as the protagonist and, in so doing, transformed the great philosopher into a legendary figure. Xenophon's portrait is the only one other than Plato's to survive, and while it offers a very personal interpretation of Socratic thought, it also reveals much about the man and his philosophical views. In 'Socrates' Defence' Xenophon defends his mentor against charges of arrogance made at his trial, while the 'Memoirs of Socrates' also starts with an impassioned plea for the rehabilitation of a wronged reputation. Along with 'The Estate-Manager', a practical economic treatise, and 'The Dinner-Party', a sparkling exploration of love, Xenophon's dialogues offer fascinating insights into the Socratic world and into the intellectual atmosphere and daily life of ancient Greece.

Xenophon's complete Socratic works are translated in this volume. In his introduction, Robin Waterfield illuminates the significance of these four books, showing how perfectly they embody the founding principles of Socratic thought.

Translated by Hugh Tredennick and Robin Waterfield and edited with new material by Robin Waterfield

PENGUIN CLASSICS

A SHORT ACCOUNT OF THE DESTRUCTION OF THE INDIES
BARTOLOMÉ DE LAS CASAS

'Oh, would that I could describe even one hundredth part of the afflictions and calamities wrought among these innocent people by the benighted Spanish!'

Bartolomé de Las Casas was the first and fiercest critic of Spanish colonialism in the New World. An early traveller to the Americas who sailed on one of Columbus's voyages, Las Casas was so horrified by the wholesale massacre he witnessed that he dedicated his life to protecting the Indian community. He wrote *A Short Account of the Destruction of the Indies* in 1542, a shocking catalogue of mass slaughter, torture and slavery, which showed that the evangelizing vision of Columbus had descended under later conquistadors into genocide. Dedicated to Philip II to alert the Castilian Crown to these atrocities and demand that the Indians be entitled to the basic rights of humankind, this passionate work of documentary vividness outraged Europe and contributed to the idea of the Spanish 'Black Legend' that would last for centuries.

Nigel Griffin's powerful translation conveys the compelling immediacy of Las Casas's writing. This edition also contains an introduction discussing his life, work and political legacy.

Translated by Nigel Griffin with an introduction by Anthony Pagden

PENGUIN CLASSICS

PARADISE LOST
JOHN MILTON

'Better to reign in Hell, than serve in Heav'n ...'

In *Paradise Lost* Milton produced a poem of epic scale, conjuring up a vast, awe-inspiring cosmos and ranging across huge tracts of space and time. And yet, in putting a charismatic Satan and naked Adam and Eve at the centre of this story, he also created an intensely human tragedy on the Fall of Man. Written when Milton was in his fifties – blind, bitterly disappointed by the Restoration and briefly in danger of execution – *Paradise Lost*'s apparent ambivalence towards authority has led to intense debate about whether it manages to 'justify the ways of God to men', or exposes the cruelty of Christianity.

John Leonard's revised edition of *Paradise Lost* contains full notes, elucidating Milton's biblical, classical and historical allusions and discussing his vivid, highly original use of language and blank verse.

'An endless moral maze, introducing literature's first Romantic, Satan' John Carey

Edited with an introduction and notes by John Leonard